MEDITERRANEAN DIET COOKBOOK
For Beginners 2022

CHRISTINE CONSOLMAGNO

Copyright - 2022 - All rights reserved.

The content contained within this book may not be reproduced, duplicated or transmitted without direct written permission from the author or the publisher.

Under no circumstances will any blame or legal responsibility be held against the publisher, or author, for any damages, reparation, or monetary loss due to the information contained within this book. Either directly or indirectly.

Legal Notice:

This book is copyright protected. This book is only for personal use. You cannot amend, distribute, sell, use, quote or paraphrase any part, or the content within this book, without the consent of the author or publisher.

Disclaimer Notice:

Please note the information contained within this document is for educational and entertainment purposes only. All effort has been executed to present accurate, up to date, and reliable, complete information. No warranties of any kind are declared or implied. Readers acknowledge that the author is not engaging in the rendering of legal, financial, medical or professional advice. The content within this book has been derived from various sources. Please consult a licensed professional before attempting any techniques outlined in this book.

By reading this document, the reader agrees that under no circumstances is the author responsible for any losses, direct or indirect, which are incurred as a result of the use of information contained within this document, including, but not limited to, - errors, omissions, or inaccuracies.

TABLE OF CONTENTS

INTRODUCTION   9

CHAPTER 1
WHAT IS MEDITERRANEAN DIET   15

CHAPTER 2
MEDITERRANEAN DIET PYRAMID   21

CHAPTER 3
MEAL PLAN   29

CHAPTER 4
BREAKFAST RECIPES   35
- 1. Bacon and Cream Cheese Mug Muffins   36
- 2. Cinnamon and Pecan Porridge   36
- 3. Dinosaur Eggs   37
- 4. Dill and Tomato Frittata   37
- 5. Paleo Almond Banana Pancakes   38
- 6. Zucchini with Egg   38
- 7. Cheesy Amish Breakfast Casserole   39
- 8. Breakfast Couscous   39
- 9. Avocado and Apple Smoothie   40
- 10. Mini Frittatas   40
- 11. Italian Breakfast Sausage with Baby Potatoes and Vegetables   41
- 12. Blueberry Greek Yogurt Pancakes   41
- 13. Pastry-Less Spanakopita   42
- 14. Date and Walnut Overnight Oats   42
- 15. Pear and Mango Smoothie   43
- 16. Greek Yogurt with Berries and Seeds   43
- 17. Mediterranean Breakfast Egg White Sandwich   44
- 18. Breakfast Taco Scramble   45
- 19. Cauliflower Fritters with Hummus   46
- 20. Overnight Berry Chia Oats   47
- 21. Feta and Quinoa Egg Muffins   47
- 22. 5-Minute Heirloom Tomato and Cucumber Toast   48
- 23. Garlic Parmesan Chicken Wings   48

24. Feta Avocado and Mashed Chickpea Toast ... 49
25. Pilaf with Cream Cheese ... 49
26. Easy Spaghetti Squash ... 50
27. Creamy Mango and Banana Overnight Oats ... 51
28. Bacon and Eggs with Tomatoes ... 51
29. Sun-Dried Tomatoes Oatmeal ... 52
30. Breakfast Egg on Avocado ... 52
31. Potato Scallops with Truffle Oil ... 53
32. Mediterranean Pasta with Basil ... 53
33. Brekky Egg-Potato Hash ... 54
34. Cinnamon Porridge ... 54
35. Cherry Smoothie Bowl ... 55

CHAPTER 5
LUNCH RECIPES ... 57

36. Grilled Pesto Salmon with Asparagus ... 58
37. Cheddar-Stuffed Burgers with Zucchini ... 58
38. Chicken Cordon Bleu with Cauliflower ... 59
39. Rosemary Roasted Pork with Cauliflower ... 59
40. Chicken Tikka with Cauliflower Rice ... 60
41. Beef and Broccoli Stir-Fry ... 60
42. Parmesan-Crusted Halibut with Asparagus ... 61
43. Hearty Beef and Bacon Casserole ... 61
44. Sesame Wings with Cauliflower ... 62
45. Baked Zucchini Noodles with Feta ... 62
46. Brussels Sprouts with Bacon ... 63
47. Bun less Burger-Keto Style ... 63
48. Coffee BBQ Pork Belly ... 64
49. Garlic and Thyme Lamb Chops ... 64
50. Jamaican Jerk Pork Roast ... 65
51. Mixed Vegetable Patties-Instant Pot ... 65
52. Roasted Leg of Lamb ... 66
53. Salmon Pasta ... 66
54. Skillet Fried Cod ... 67
55. Slow-Cooked Kalua Pork and Cabbage ... 67
56. Steak Pinwheels ... 68
57. Tangy Shrimp ... 68
58. Beef and Broccoli Roast ... 69
59. Fried Green Beans Rosemary ... 69
60. Crispy Broccoli Pop Corn ... 70
61. Cheesy Cauliflower Croquettes ... 70
62. Spinach in Cheese Envelopes ... 71
63. Cheesy Mushroom Slices ... 71

64. Asparagus Fries ... 72
65. Kale Chips ... 72
66. Guacamole ... 73
67. Zucchini Noodles ... 73
68. Cauliflower soufflé ... 74
69. Banana Waffles ... 74
70. Turkey Burgers with Mango Salsa ... 75

CHAPTER 6
DINNER RECIPES ... 77
71. Ritzy Veggie Chili ... 78
72. Spicy Italian Bean Balls with Marinara ... 79
73. Baked Rolled Oat with Pears and Pecans ... 80
74. Greek Green Beans ... 80
75. Spicy Zucchini ... 81
76. Carrot Potato Medley ... 81
77. Flavors Basil Lemon Ratatouille ... 82
78. Feta Green Beans ... 82
79. Delicious Pepper Zucchini ... 83
80. Lemon Artichokes ... 83
81. Delicious Okra ... 84
82. Parsnips with Eggplant ... 84
83. Eggplant with Olives ... 85
84. Zucchini, Tomato, Potato Ratatouille ... 85
85. Tomato Stuffed with Cheese and Peppers ... 86
86. Loaded Portobello Mushrooms ... 86
87. Sumac Chicken with Cauliflower and Carrots ... 87
88. Harissa Yogurt Chicken Thighs ... 87
89. Braised Chicken with Wild Mushrooms ... 88
90. Braised Duck with Fennel Root ... 88
91. Chicken Gyros with Tzatziki ... 89
92. Eggplant Casserole ... 90
93. Dijon and Herb Pork Tenderloin ... 91
94. Steak with Red Wine-Mushroom Sauce ... 92
95. Greek Meatballs ... 93
96. Lamb with String Beans ... 93
97. Fish Fillet on Lemons ... 94
98. Tilapia Fillet with Onion and Avocado ... 95
99. Sea Bass Crusted with Moroccan Spices ... 96
100. Classic Escabeche ... 97
101. Thyme Whole Roasted Red Snapper ... 98
102. Crispy Fried Sardines ... 98
103. Fish and Orzo ... 99

104. Spiced Soup with Lentils and Legumes	99
105. Brown Rice Pilaf with Golden Raisins	100

CHAPTER 7
SNACK RECIPES — 101

106. Mediterranean Pasta	102
107. Nonna's Spaghetti and Broccoli	103
108. One-Pot Creamy Hummus Pasta	103
109. Ingredient Chicken Feta Pasta	104
110. One-Pot Creamy Tuscan Garlic Spaghetti	105
111. 10-Minute Mediterranean Vegan Pasta	105
112. Best Vegan Chili with Quinoa	106
113. Shrimp Pasta with Lemon Garlic Sauce	107
114. One-Pot Spinach and Feta Macaroni and Cheese	108
115. One-Pot Buffalo Chicken Pasta	108
116. Drunken Wild Mushroom Pasta	109
117. Shrimp Spaghetti Aglio Olio	110
118. 15-Minute Caprese Pasta Recipe	110
119. Mediterranean One-Pot Pasta	111
120. Farfalle with Tuna, Lemon, and Fennel	112
121. Easy Italian Shrimp Tortellini Bake	112
122. Pasta Fagioli	113
123. Sweet Potato Noodles with Almond Sauce	114
124. Shrimp and Pasta Stew	115
125. Cold Lemon Zoodles	115
126. Pasta Alla Norma with Eggplant, Basil and Pecorino	116
127. Tortellini with Pesto and Broccoli	117
128. Spinach Pesto Pasta	117
129. Authentic Pasta e Fagioli	118
130. Chicken Spinach and Artichoke Stuffed Spaghetti Squash	119
131. Angel Hair with Asparagus-Kale Pesto	120
132. Spicy Pasta Puttanesca	120
133. Chicken Pizza	121
134. Spinach and Feta Pita Bake	121
135. Beef Pizza	122
136. Shrimp Pizza	123
137. Veggie Pizza	123
138. Watermelon Feta and Balsamic Pizza	124
139. White Pizza with Prosciutto and Arugula	124
140. Za'atar Pizza	125

CHAPTER 8
DESSERT RECIPES 127

- 141. Traditional Olive Oil Cake with Figs — 128
- 142. Mascarpone and Fig Crostini — 128
- 143. Traditional Mediterranean Lokum — 129
- 144. Mixed Berry and Fig Compote — 129
- 145. Creamed Fruit Salad — 130
- 146. Almond Cookies — 130
- 147. Crunchy Sesame Cookies — 131
- 148. Mini Orange Tarts — 131
- 149. Traditional Kalo Prama — 132
- 150. Turkish-Style Chocolate Halva — 132
- 151. Rice Pudding with Dried Figs — 133
- 152. Fruit Kabobs with Yogurt Deep — 133
- 153. Stuffed Dried Figs — 134
- 154. Feta Cheesecake — 134
- 155. No-Bake Chocolate Squares — 135
- 156. Greek Parfait with Mixed Berries — 135
- 157. Greek-Style Chocolate Semifreddo — 136
- 158. Traditional Italian Cake with Almonds — 137
- 159. Pear Croustade — 137
- 160. Loukoumades (Fried Honey Balls) — 138
- 161. Crème Caramel — 138
- 162. Galaktoboureko — 139
- 163. Kourabiedes Almond Cookies — 139
- 164. Revani Syrup Cake — 140
- 165. Almonds and Oats Pudding — 140
- 166. Mediterranean Tomato Salad with Feta and Fresh Herbs — 141
- 167. Quinoa Bowl with Yogurt, Dates, and Almonds — 141
- 168. Almond Butter Banana Chocolate Smoothie — 142
- 169. Maple Vanilla Baked Pears — 142
- 170. Easy Roasted Fruit Recipe — 143
- 171. Triple Chocolate Tiramisu — 143
- 172. Easy Strawberry Crepes Recipe — 144
- 173. Dried Fruit Compote — 145
- 174. Chocolate Rice Pudding — 145
- 175. Fruit Compote — 146

INDEX 147

CONCLUSION 151

Introduction

A Mediterranean diet has been initially developed in Greece and Southern Italy. Typical components of the Mediterranean diet are fruits, vegetables, whole grains, beans, nuts, and seeds such as olive or canola oil. Whole grains are also a healthy part of any well-balanced diet.

The objective behind this type of diet is to lower your heart disease risk and help you maintain health during aging; it's also known for being low in saturated fats. The Mediterranean diet is one of the best eating habits because of its high nutritional value and low-calorie consumption.

The Mediterranean diet is full of never-ending varieties of healthy, fresh, and delicious foods. However, there is more of an emphasis on certain types of foods; nothing is excluded. Therefore, people who try a Mediterranean diet can enjoy the dishes they love while also learning to appreciate how good the freshest, healthiest foods can be.

Transitioning into the Mediterranean diet is mainly about bracing yourself for a new way of eating, adapting your attitude toward food into one of joyful expectation and appreciation of good meals and good company. It's like a mindset like anything else, so you'll want to make your environment unite so you can quickly adapt to the lifestyle in the Mediterranean way.

The Scientific Reviews about Mediterranean Diet Is Impressive

"The studies suggest that the Mediterranean diet may be one of the healthiest diets for a long and healthy life."—The American Journal of Clinical Nutrition.

For centuries, the Mediterranean diet has been hailed by doctors and nutritionists as among the healthiest in the world. Here are 6 reasons why:

It's high in plant food and low on animal products. This Mediterranean diet is rich in plant-based foods, including salads, fruits, nuts, and beans. It's also low in meat and dairy products. So what foods are high in plant protein? Good ones include dark green vegetables like spinach and kale, Plum and prunes, Lentils, Walnuts, Nuts (almonds, pistachios, walnuts), and cheese (cow's milk cheese is best). Another point to remember: A diet high in protein can interfere with calcium absorption.

It's based on a lot of olive oil. Some think the Mediterranean diet is all butter and oil, but it's not. Olive oil is high in monounsaturated fat, which has been proven to reduce blood pressure and LDL cholesterol and increase HDL cholesterol.

It's high in fiber. Fiber can help lower blood pressure, and according to a study from the University of Maryland Medical Center, fiber can also help protect against some cancers—especially colon cancer.

It's rich in antioxidants. This Mediterranean diet is rich in antioxidants, which can help your immune system fight off diseases and fight cancer.

It's got more omega-3s than any diet before it. Research has shown that omega-3 fatty acids—particularly alpha-linoleic acid (found in flaxseed oil)—are crucial to good health and may help prevent or treat heart disease, certain cancers, arthritis, obesity, and other ailments that are associated with inflammation.

It helps prevent obesity. One recent study followed almost 15,000 people from 9 countries over 4 years and found that those who ate Mediterranean style were less likely to become obese than other diets.

The Mediterranean diet is generally high in fruits, vegetables, and fish but low in red meat and dairy products. It can be adapted to any diet: vegan, vegetarian, pescetarian (eating fish), or anyone who just wants to improve their eating habits.

History and Origins of the Diet

The first observational study that led to elaborating the concept of the "Mediterranean diet" and understanding its benefits, which became famous as the 7 Countries Study, was conducted by the American biologist and physiologist Ancel Keys in the 1940s.

Keys, who was in Crete at the time following allied troops, noted that the incidence of cardiovascular disease on the island was much lower than in the United States. After several years, in 1944, in Paestum, he made the same observation about the population of Cilento and guessed that the low incidence of heart disease could be related to diet.

He moved to Pioppi, a village of Cilento, where he could better observe the diet of the local people: he noticed farmers of the small towns of Southern Italy had a diet poor in fats of animal origin and mainly made of bread and pasta or soups, often consumed with legumes, seasonal fruits and vegetables of their gardens, extra-virgin olive oil, cheese, dried fruits, and wine. Habits that, both for the peasants of Cilento and the inhabitants of Crete Island, resulted in higher longevity and a lower incidence of cardiovascular diseases than the ones observed in the citizens of Northern Europe and the United States of America.

In the 1950s, people started to move away from the prairie-style diet of meat and potatoes popular for centuries. This new cuisine, which became known as the Mediterranean diet or Mediterranean way of eating, was initially seen in Italy (particularly among Italians living in villages near Naples).

A typical Mediterranean diet includes many fruits, vegetables, whole grains, olive oil, and fish but very little sugar. Seafood is common, but red meat isn't a staple of these menus. Wine can be consumed, but it's usually consumed with meals rather than by itself because Mediterranean cultures see alcohol as part of a healthy lifestyle instead of abuse. Therefore, red wine is typically consumed with meals or during the main course of the meal. Beer and spirits are almost unheard of. Snacks are also eaten at this time; these may include nuts but often have more prepackaged foods like a bread roll with olive oil or smaller portions that can be eaten for the day, like boiled eggs and vegetables.

Foods from both the Mediterranean region and Italy were featured as part of the "Eat More Color" campaign in 1985 to inform people about the importance of fruits and vegetables.

The Mediterranean diet is based on a healthy balance of fat from olive oil, fish, nuts, and other plant sources. In addition, there is high consumption of legumes and omega-3 fatty acids. This diet may also benefit heart health as people commonly have low levels of bad cholesterol (LDL). The Mediterranean diet isn't just about the food that's eaten but also about an overall lifestyle. The social aspect is considered very important, with regular family meals and gatherings around big tables being common. People don't tend to snack between meals or eat processed foods very often since it has been grasped that this is not part of traditional eating in these areas.

There is an accurate weight of evidence that demonstrates the health benefits of Mediterranean eating. For example, it has been shown that the Mediterranean diet can have positive effects on cholesterol. Eating a Mediterranean diet can significantly lower LDL (bad) cholesterol and triglycerides and raise HDL (good) cholesterol associated with a reduced risk of developing heart disease.

More than 10,000 recipes for Mediterranean dishes, most of which date from before the 17th century. The best known are those from Tuscany, Lazio, Sicily, and Sardinia. Other regions include Calabria, Abruzzo, Emilia-Romagna, and Friuli-Venezia Giulia. These dishes are simple and rustic but generally very flavorful. There is usually plenty of olive oil, fresh herbs, and tomatoes. Meat is not typically eaten in these regions. But the typical Mediterranean diet does include fish or seafood twice per week as part of a healthful diet.

The traditional cuisine of Southern Italy is reflected in its wines, with wines made from the Tuscany grape and many protected names on the wine label, such as Chianti Classico and Brunello di Montalcino.

The Mediterranean diet (Diet of the Mediterranean) is low in fat and moderate in carbs and describes a diet with a wide range of fruits, vegetables, legumes, cereals, and nuts. This diet aims to improve the heart's health and decrease the risks of various chronic diseases for both men and women, especially chronic kidney diseases (CKD), cancers, and diabetes.

Currently, numerous studies are showing that Mediterranean diets have many health benefits. For example, one review concluded that: "Overall, Mediterranean-style diets implemented ad libitum are associated with lower all-cause mortality rates compared with other dietary patterns. These observations may have important public health implications."

The Mediterranean diet as a way of eating is highly successful and significantly lowers heart problems, obesity, and diabetes. A review of 53 trials in 2015 concluded that 93 out of 144 interventions showed positive results for the Mediterranean diet overall, with the benefits particularly striking for cardiovascular disease. However, the study also found that only 15% of those who try to follow a Mediterranean-style diet can stick to it for more than a year.

One 2015 meta-analysis found that people who consume diets high in plant-based foods such as fruits and vegetables, legumes, and nuts are less likely to develop heart disease than people who regularly eat red meat or dairy products.

Another meta-analysis found that a Mediterranean-style diet generally lowers blood pressure and in some cases, cholesterol.

A review of the Mediterranean diet for diabetes management found that it effectively reduced symptoms of diabetes and improved glucose control over time.

The Greek Island of Crete has been shown to have a high rate of cognitive preservation in older adults, possibly due to the popular diet used for at least 6,000 years, which is high in tomato products, vegetables, and legumes.

The diet is also high in garlic.

According to Antonella Sforza, the Mediterranean diet and a healthy lifestyle are not incompatible. The Italian diet consists mainly of fruits, vegetables, whole grains, legumes, lean meat, and fish; it is low in dairy products and rich in olive oil. A healthy Mediterranean-style diet can be adopted by people with diabetes, along with a healthy lifestyle.

Increasing nutritional awareness has been associated with an increased interest in the Mediterranean diet, resulting in more people preparing it at home and consuming it daily. In Spain, the number of stores selling health foods and organic products such as olive oil has increased steadily over the last decade.

The Mediterranean diet is linked to the economic performance of each country in the Mediterranean area. Thus, there are reasons to believe that the Mediterranean diet is a valuable treasure for these countries, and some reasons are its social, health, and economic benefits.

The positive impact of the Mediterranean diet on physical health is well documented, but there is also a growing awareness regarding the influence of this pattern on mental health. The psychological state of people adhering to this dietary pattern has been reported as improved after 2 weeks. On a psychological level, results have been observed regarding increased self-esteem, well-being, and optimism; also, reduced loneliness was noted together with less anxiety, depression, and irritability.

CHAPTER 1

What is mediterranean diet

When someone hears the words "Mediterranean diet," what comes to mind is chicken, fish, and tomatoes. There are also many different variables in a Mediterranean-style diet that can vary from country to country.

One of these factors includes olive oil as a key part of the Mediterranean diet. Those who follow this style of eating usually consume some type of olive oil daily as their main source of fat intake with other vegetable oils such as sunflower or rapeseed oil in smaller amounts. It is in the Mediterranean climate that people first began to use olive oil for cooking and producing olive oil.

The word "olive" now comes from the Greek "olivos," which means "of the olive tree" or "from olives," which refers to olives grown in an area close by. The olives themselves vary from small and round to large and oval, with a sharp point on the end. When it comes down to its culinary use, just about anything can be done with olive oil. There is a traditional Greek way of using it as a dressing for salads or as a dipping sauce for vegetables and bread, but other uses are still being developed.

There are also over 50 types of bread and pasta being made in the Mediterranean region. These foods include pitas, tortillas, couscous, bulgur wheat, farina, barley, pasta, and others.

Another unique factor of the Mediterranean way is the type of meats used in their diet. In Southern Europe, it is more common to see poultry and fish preparations than beef or pork dishes, but in Northern Europe, it is more common to see these types of meats in their diet. Another group that tends to eat beef and pork is in Turkey.

Although the Mediterranean diet is known for its use of olive oil, it also includes a lot of fresh vegetables such as tomatoes, peppers, potatoes, and onions. Fruits are also an important part of the Mediterranean diet, but they should not be consumed every day because they are high in sugar content. This diet is also known for its usage of herbs and spices such as rosemary, basil, oregano, mints, cilantro, and parsley. These ingredients are used to enhance the flavor of many different foods; including soups or stews.

While evidence remains inconclusive whether adherence to a Mediterranean diet confers additional health benefits beyond those conferred by a healthy lifestyle, the traditional Mediterranean diet was mainly recommended for its ability to promote healthy living among people already living with a disease. The term was first introduced in 1992 by Walter Willett from Harvard School of Public Health in Boston during a lecture at WHO headquarters. Even though the Mediterranean diet was originally a term used by the European Union (EU) to promote healthy living, it has since been taken up by health-conscious people in other parts of the world.

Benefits of the Mediterranean Diet

The Mediterranean diet is a method for eating and a lifestyle shared by the individuals of the Mediterranean locale.

Every one of the 16 countries that make up the Mediterranean coast feed also, although they may offer some various highlights relying upon the area and culture.

As a rule term, the Mediterranean diet is described by the bounty and decent variety of plants (for example, natural products, vegetables, oats, and fruits), the consumption of olive oil for cooking and dressing, fish, low-fat dairy, and moderate wine consumption.

Benefits given by the Mediterranean diet have been contemplated in the course of the only remaining century due to the solid status that the occupants of this area appear to appreciate, with a presumed lower frequency of certain diseases.

The properties of this diet were found by a researcher from abroad in this district, who figured out how to see the benefits of this eating style.

Mediterranean Diet for Cardiovascular Well-Being

The Mediterranean diet is especially advantageous for the heart and circulatory framework.

Its benefits are expected in huge part to the bounty of vegetables, high fiber, and cancer prevention agent mixes, and the nearness of solid fats omega-3, 6, and 9 in impeccable equalization.

- **Reduce hypertension:** The Mediterranean diet assists to control blood pressure. It is one of the meal plans prescribed for hypertension. Its belongings are because of the nearness of solid fats and the consumption of onions and garlic copious with antihypertensive properties.
- **Improve cholesterol levels:** The nearness of omega fats in the diet, nuts, olive oil, and slick fish help lower bad cholesterol. It additionally aids the procedure of fiber consumption from vegetables.
- **Prevents atherosclerosis:** The Mediterranean diet is wealthy in cell reinforcements, which forestall cholesterol development in the veins. It likewise builds good cholesterol, in this manner diminishing the danger of atherosclerosis.

Include vegetable foods wealthy in omega-3.

Olive oil and dry nuts don't raise cholesterol levels.

- Improves course: Olive oil diminishes the danger of thrombosis, and vegetable plants have parts that improve circulation, such as the lycopene found in tomatoes and peppers.

The Mediterranean diet diminishes up to 30% of the danger of cardiovascular disease.

The Mediterranean Diet Likewise Benefits the Pneumonic Framework

As exhibited by logical investigations, the Mediterranean diet reduces the danger of lung disease.

These properties are because this diet is rich in vitamins, remarkably nutrient E from olive oil, and nutrient C from vegetables, just as solid fat and phytochemicals.

The additional virgin olive oil has antimicrobial and mitigating power, which ensures us against respiratory diseases, hypersensitivities, and asthma.

In an investigation on youngsters in Crete, it was indicated that normal consumption of the new natural product, alongside the Mediterranean dietary propensities, helps treat the manifestations of asthma and rhinitis. It is noticed that among Crete's populace, there is a low pace of unfavorably susceptible side effects.

Another examination recommends that the Mediterranean diet parts the danger of incessant obstructive pneumonic disease, even in smokers.

Mediterranean Diet Improves Diabetes

The Mediterranean diet lessens the danger of diabetes-related diseases, for example, cholesterol or hypertension. The transcendence of vegetables in this diet controls glucose levels, decreases cholesterol, advances flow, and forestalls hairlike delicacy.

Nonetheless, in the Mediterranean diet for diabetics, some dietary viewpoints ought to be adjusted so as to improve the resilience to the diet.

Mediterranean Diet for Alzheimer

The Mediterranean diet is related to a lower danger of Alzheimer's disease.

Because of the plenitude of consumption of vegetables and olive oil, it is a diet that improves blood supply to the mind with high potential and cancer prevention agent properties.

The Mediterranean diet has neuroprotective impacts against mind stroke, Huntington's disease, Alzheimer's disease, numerous sclerosis, Parkinson's disease, feeble dementia, and fringe neuropathy.

Mediterranean Diet Improves Intellectual Capacities

Image of nuts, a wellspring of sound omega fats for your cerebrum.

The commitment of cell reinforcements which the Mediterranean diet gloats about, for example, in vegetables and olive oil, improves subjective capacities and improves memory, as logical investigations have appeared.

It is an entirely reasonable diet for individuals with stress, understudies, or individuals with memory misfortune at a mature age.

The Mediterranean Diet Allows the Correct Improvement of Development

The Mediterranean diet is wealthy in iodine because of the consumption of fish and seafood routinely in the diet. Iodine is a fundamental mineral for the working of the thyroid organ, which directs body digestion.

Its deficiency is related to disease and development issues, for example, goiter and cretinism, or mental impediment.

The iodine consumption in the sound Mediterranean diet from fish is an assurance of development and full physical and mental improvement.

The worldwide worry about iodine lack brought about table salt advancement with this mineral (iodized salt), which has figured out how to address iodine nutritional insufficiencies in numerous populaces, where seafood consumption is low.

It is likewise a diet containing milk, wealthy in calcium, which advances the full improvement of bone structure, sets solid bones, and forestalls osteoporosis.

Creature meat is a less copious food supply. Its quality in the diet is all around portrayed by the following saying, "Recollect meat as a topping and not as food!" For sure, the customary Mediterranean diet is a long way from the abundance of carnivorism, which can cause bone decalcification.

Testimonies of People Who Have Tried Mediterranean Diet

Anyone who has tried to lose weight using the Mediterranean diet knows that it can be quite challenging. And yet, despite the difficulties and challenges associated with this eating plan, some people have found success with it. This book provides you with five testimonies of people who have tried this diet and succeeded in their weight loss goals. It also highlights how incorporating healthy fats can help to maintain a healthier lifestyle.

The testimonials shared here come from five varied individuals who were able to incorporate different elements of the Mediterranean diet into their daily lives while still enjoying bread, pasta, steak, and occasional desserts (in moderation, of course).

The first is from Mollie, who had a great sense of humor about her experience:

"As you can see, I really don't have much of a waist to show off anymore. That's because I followed the Mediterranean diet and went from 228 pounds to 152 pounds in just 3 months! I love my new figure, and all my friends say I look 10 years younger. What's even better is that the weight loss was effortless because eating right really can be delicious. For example, each morning during breakfast, instead of regular toast or bagels, I eat a big bowl of fresh fruit salad. This tasty treat is loaded with fiber and antioxidants. And I love it! And if I'm feeling a bit peckish during the afternoon, I eat an apple with peanut butter. Oh, and if my sweet tooth gets the best of me, I'll just have a few almonds."

Nutty Nora lost 100 pounds in 6 months on the Mediterranean diet. She's here to tell us how:

"I followed this diet religiously and ended up losing a total of 100 pounds in 6 months. The Mediterranean plan was very easy for me because I love cheese and eggs so much. My favorite snack is a nice big bowl of scrambled eggs with lots of mozzarella cheese melted right on top. And I can't get enough of my homemade pesto sauce, which I spread on a plate of spaghetti with lots of melted cheese. All the carbs in this diet made it easy for me to fulfill my voracious appetite. I just love bread, pasta, and even rice with butter. And for dessert, I love a nice big piece of cake or pie!"

Susie's testimonial about following a Mediterranean diet is quite inspiring. She lost 55 pounds in 3 months:

"I loved how easy it was to get started on this diet and start losing weight immediately. For example, I always used to dip my bread in olive oil and balsamic vinegar when eating at restaurants. And eating lots of bread and pasta made it easy for me to fulfill my hunger. And I could enjoy a delicious piece of chocolate cake or ice cream after dinner, but in moderation, of course."

James tells us about the ease he found in following a Mediterranean diet:

"I had been under-eating for years, trying to lose a few pounds here and there. But now I feel like a completely different person… literally. I really do look better than I have in years, and it's all thanks to this diet I'm following. It's probably hard to believe that an Italian diet could help someone like me, but it really did. I don't have to give up my favorite foods anymore, and I still feel full for hours after eating."

Judy lost 60 pounds in 10 weeks on the Mediterranean diet. She says, "I am already down about 20 pounds. I love this diet!"

"From the first day that I started following this diet, I found it very easy to follow. My favorite dishes are pasta with pesto sauce, lamb chops with a salad, and grilled salmon filets. And if my appetite is really raging, I'll just go ahead and eat some cheese or olives… in moderation, of course! Thank you, Mediterranean Diet! By following the Mediterranean plan, you can lose weight without depriving yourself of your favorite foods."

CHAPTER 2

Mediterranean diet pyramid

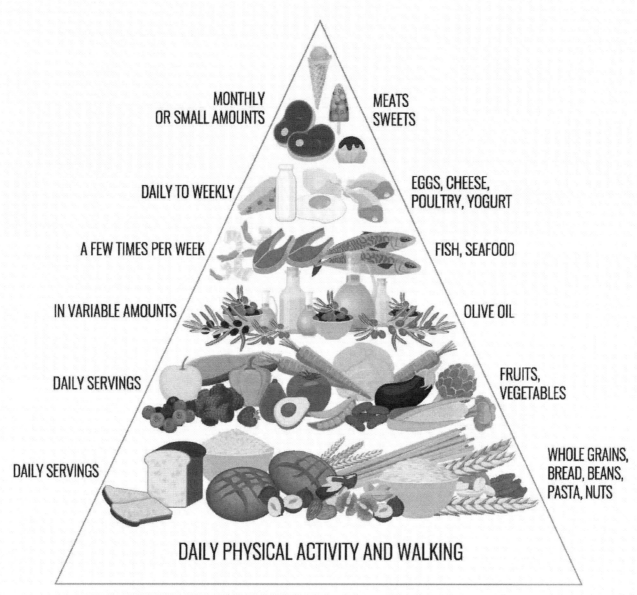

The Mediterranean diet Pyramid is a nutritional guide developed by the World Health Organization, Harvard School of Public Health, and Oldways Preservation Trust in 1993. It is a visual tool that summarizes the Mediterranean diet, suggests eating patterns, and guides how frequently specific mechanisms should be eaten. It allows you to break healthy eating habits and not overfill yourself with too many calories.

- **Olive oil, fruits, vegetables, whole grains, legumes, beans, nuts and seeds, spices, and herbs.** These foods form the Mediterranean pyramid base. If you did observe, you would notice that these are primarily from plant sources. You should try and include a few variations of these items into each meal you eat. Olive oil should be the primary fat in cooking your dishes and endeavor to replace any other butter or cooking oil you may have been using to cook.
- **Fish and seafood.** These are essential staples of the Mediterranean diet that should be consumed often as a protein source. You would want to include these in your diet at least 2 times a week. Try new varieties of fish, either frozen or fresh. Also, incorporate seafood like mussels, crab, and shrimp into your diet. Canned tuna is also great to include on sandwiches or toss in a salad with fresh vegetables.
- **Cheese, yogurt, eggs, and poultry.** These ingredients should be consumed in more moderate amounts. Depending on the food, they should be used sparingly throughout the week. Keep in mind that they will also be counted in your weekly limit if you are using eggs in baking or cooking. You would want to stick to more healthy cheese like Parmesan, Ricotta, or Feta that you can add a topping or garnish on your dishes.
- **Red meat and sweets.** These items are going to be consumed less frequently. If you are going to eat them, you need to consume only small quantities, most preferably lean meat versions with less fat when possible. Most studies recommend a maximum of 12–16 oz per month. To add more variety to your diet, you can still have red meat occasionally, but you would want to reduce how often you have it. It is essential to limit its intake because of all the health concerns of sugar and red meat. The Mediterranean diet improves cardiovascular health and reduces blood pressure, while red meat tends to be dangerous to your cardiovascular system. The Greece population ate very little red meat and instead had fish or seafood as their primary protein source.
- **Water.** The Mediterranean diet encourages you to stay hydrated at all times. It means drinking more water than your daily intake. The Institute of Medicine recommends a total of 9 cups each day for women and 13 cups for men. For pregnant or breastfeeding women, the number should be increased.
- **Wine.** Moderate consumption of wine with meals is encouraged on the Mediterranean diet. Studies have shown that moderate consumption of alcohol can reduce the risk of heart disease. That can mean about 1 glass per day for women. Men tend to have higher body mass so that they can consume 1 to 2 drinks. Please keep in mind what your doctor would recommend regarding wine consumption based on your health and family history.

The Foods of the Mediterranean Diet and Serving Score

Here is what your typical daily diet should look like:

Fresh Fruits and Vegetables: Unlimited, but at Least 4 Servings Per Day

Devouring your fruits and vegetables raw is excellent, but steamed, roasted, sautéed, poached, grilled, and baked fruits and vegetables are all welcome on the Mediterranean diet. Avoid boiling vegetables, as many of the nutrients are lost in the water, and the result is far less flavorful and colorful than with other cooking methods. Use olive oil and herbs in the preparation rather than butter and excessive salt.

Whole Grains: 3–5 Servings Per Day

Whole grains are an integral part of the Mediterranean diet and part of why the diet is so rich in heart-healthful fiber. So, forgo white bread and overly processed grain products and focus on whole grains such as whole wheat, oats, barley, and brown rice.

Healthful Fats: 4–6 Servings Per Day

Healthful fats are an essential part of the Mediterranean diet. Get them from olive oil, olives, avocados, fresh fish, shellfish, nuts, and seeds.

Fish and Seafood: At Least 3 Servings Per Week

Cold-water fishes with the highest omega-3 fats are sardines, haddock, mackerel, cod, and salmon. You may also include shellfish like clams, shrimp, lobster, mussels, oysters, and crab.

Dairy Products: Up to 7 Servings Per Week

Milk, yogurt, and cheese are welcome on the Mediterranean diet. Choose low-fat cheeses and milk and opt for Greek yogurt whenever possible, as it contains twice the protein of regular yogurt. Generally, milk is reserved for cereal, coffee or tea, and baking. Cheese is used as a dessert or flavoring for soups, salads, entrées, and cheese sauces, which are not a regular part of the Mediterranean diet.

Eggs: 3–5 Servings (of 2 Eggs Each) Per Week

Eggs are traditionally enjoyed frequently in the Mediterranean diet, especially by those families that raise their chickens. Opt for organic, free-range, hormone-free eggs. They're safer and contain more omega-3 fats than commercial eggs. Use them for baking, in sauces, and as entrées.

Poultry: 2–5 Servings Per Week

Poultry is eaten far more often in the Mediterranean than red meat. You can eat any cuts of chicken and turkey, although it's recommended that you remove the skin and any visible fat before eating. Game birds are also welcome on a diet, so you can choose quail, duck, pheasant, pigeon, or any other bird that you like.

Sweets: Up to 4 Servings Per Week

Although the Mediterranean people enjoy sweets, dessert is typically cheese and/or fruit, not sugary pastries. Go for fruit most of the week and reserve sweeter desserts for special meals with guests or as an occasional treat. Artificial sweeteners are not recommended; instead, stick with sugar, honey, and molasses in small quantities.

Red Meat: 3–5 Servings Per Month

Red meats like beef, pork, and lamb are generally reserved for a few special meals, and portions are much smaller than most Western plates. Choose organic, grass-fed meats whenever possible (as they are higher in omega-3s), and leaner cuts such as sirloin or loin should be given preference over the fattier ones, such as bacon or ribs.

What to Eat and What to Avoid

Many countries that fit into this region are known for their health and longevity, including Italy, Spain, and Greece. In this guide, I'll share with you some recipes for what to eat on the Mediterranean diet as well as a plan based on real-life dishes from these countries.

While there are elements of it that might be considered low-carb (vegetables, beans, high-quality olive oil), this isn't a high-protein diet.

- **Only rarely eat:** Red meat.
- **Not to eat:** Sugar-sweetened beverages, added sugars, processed meats, refined grains, refined oils, and other highly processed foods.

Foods to Avoid

You must avoid these unhealthy ingredients and foods:

- Added sugar: Soft drinks, candy, table sugar, ice cream, and many others.
- White bread, refined wheat pasta, and other refined grains
- Margarine and other processed foods contain trans fats.
- Soybean oil, rapeseed oil, cottonseed oil, and other refined oils
- Processed meat: Processed sausages, hot dogs, etc.
- Highly processed foods: Everything labeled "low in fat" or "diet" or that looks like it was made in a factory.

Foods to Eat

The diet studied by most studies contains a lot of healthy plant-based foods and relatively few animal foods.

The Mediterranean lifestyle also includes regular physical activity, sharing meals with other people, and enjoying life.

You must base your diet on these healthy, unprocessed Mediterranean dishes:

- **Vegetables:** Tomatoes, broccoli, kale, spinach, onions, cauliflower, carrots, Brussels sprouts, cucumbers, etc.
- **Fruit:** Apples, bananas, oranges, pears, grapes, strawberries, dates, figs, melons, peaches, etc.
- **Nuts and seeds:** Almonds, walnuts, sunflower seeds, macadamia nuts, hazelnuts, cashews, pumpkin seeds, etc.
- **Legumes:** Beans, peas, lentils, legumes, peanuts, chickpeas, etc.
- **Tubers:** Potatoes, sweet potatoes, turnips, jam, etc.
- **Whole grains:** Whole oats, rye, brown rice, barley, maize, buckwheat, whole wheat, whole meal bread, and pasta.
- **Fish and seafood:** Salmon, sardines, trout, mackerel, tuna, shrimp, oysters, cockles, crab, mussels, etc.
- **Poultry:** Duck, chicken, turkey, etc.
- **Eggs:** Chicken, quail, and duck eggs.
- **Dairy:** Cheese, Greek yogurt, yogurt, etc.
- **Herbs and spices:** Garlic, basil, sage, mint, rosemary, nutmeg, cinnamon, pepper, etc.
- **Healthy fats:** Extra-virgin olive oil, avocados, olives, and avocado oil.

Whole foods with one ingredient are the key to good health.

Drinks to Have

Water should be your favorite drink with a Mediterranean diet.

This diet also contains moderate amounts of red wine—about 1 glass per day.

Coffee and tea are also completely acceptable, but you must avoid sugar-sweetened drinks and fruit juices that are very high in sugar.

Tips on How to Improve the Effects of the Mediterranean Diet

The Mediterranean eating regimen has been acquiring a great deal of standard consideration since it has been connected to bringing down paces of coronary illness, diabetes, and disease. In light of this, there is a lot of proof that the eating regimen is very advantageous for individuals with particular sorts of constant infection. The people who cling to this eating regimen ought to remember practice as a feature of their everyday schedule for the request to receive the most extreme well-being rewards. A couple of simple methods for fusing more actual work have been illustrated underneath.

One of the clearest ways for individuals to add more exercise into their day-by-day schedule is to add a long stroll to their wake-up routine. This could be strolling their canine, taking their youngsters to the everyday schedule strolling along city roads. The key is to accomplish something outside and get the pulse up while participating in a social movement. This can likewise assist with diminishing pressure, which has been related to specific sorts of constant sickness.

The people who can't take long strolls during the day should attempt to include day-by-day extending practices at home. Also, individuals should attempt to fuse some sort of activity into their working day in case they can, for example, use the stairwell rather than the lift. The people who have work area occupations can likewise have a go at moving at their work areas or setting up on music and moving.

The Mediterranean eating routine has been connected to bringing down paces of coronary illness, diabetes, and disease. There is additionally an abundance of examination proposing that the eating regimen is very gainful for individuals with particular sorts of ongoing illness. The normal Mediterranean eating regimen is high in organic products, vegetables, entire grains, fish, and olive oil. It has additionally been displayed to lessen the danger of type 2 diabetes and a few kinds of malignant growth, like colon disease.

Including some sort of everyday exercise ought to be a given for individuals who are on this eating regimen. This won't just add to the general medical advantages yet will likewise further develop the way that individuals look and feel. The most straightforward method for doing this is by fusing more actual work into day-by-day exercises, like going for long strolls with relatives and companions for the duration of the day.

These ideas can undoubtedly squeeze into a bustling way of life. All they require is that the individual has sufficient opportunity in their day, and moves begin immediately. They don't need any extraordinary gear and should be possible anyplace. Individuals must recall that the main piece of an activity program is consistency. It just requires a couple of moments daily to receive the rewards.

CHAPTER 3

Meal plan

8-Weeks Meal Plan (56 Days)

56 DAYS MEAL PLAN	BREAKFAST	LUNCH	DINNER
Day 1	Bacon and Cream Cheese Mug Muffins	Grilled Pesto Salmon with Asparagus	Ritzy Veggie Chili
Day 2	Cinnamon and Pecan Porridge	Cheddar-Stuffed Burgers with Zucchini	Spicy Italian Bean Balls with Marinara
Day 3	Dinosaur Eggs	Chicken Cordon Bleu with Cauliflower	Baked Rolled Oat with Pears and Pecans
Day 4	Dill and Tomato Frittata	Rosemary Roasted Pork with Cauliflower	Greek Green Beans
Day 5	Paleo Almond Banana Pancakes	Chicken Tikka with Cauliflower Rice	Spicy Zucchini
Day 6	Zucchini with Egg	Beef and Broccoli Stir-Fry	Carrot Potato Medley
Day 7	Cheesy Amish Breakfast Casserole	Parmesan-Crusted Halibut with Asparagus	Flavors Basil Lemon Ratatouille
Day 8	Breakfast Couscous	Hearty Beef and Bacon Casserole	Feta Green Beans
Day 9	Avocado and Apple Smoothie	Sesame Wings with Cauliflower	Delicious Pepper Zucchini
Day 10	Mini Frittatas	Baked Zucchini Noodles with Feta	Lemon Artichokes
Day 11	Italian Breakfast Sausage with Baby Potatoes and Vegetables	Brussels Sprouts With Bacon	Delicious Okra
Day 12	Blueberry Greek Yogurt Pancakes	Bun less Burger - Keto Style	Parsnips With Eggplant

Day 13	Pastry-Less Spanakopita	Coffee BBQ Pork Belly	Eggplant With Olives
Day 14	Date and Walnut Overnight Oats	Garlic and Thyme Lamb Chops	Zucchini Tomato Potato Ratatouille
Day 15	Pear and Mango Smoothie	Jamaican Jerk Pork Roast	Tomato Stuffed with Cheese and Peppers
Day 16	Greek Yogurt w/ Berries and Seeds	Mixed Vegetable Patties - Instant Pot	Loaded Portobello Mushrooms
Day 17	Mediterranean Breakfast Egg White Sandwich	Roasted Leg of Lamb	Sumac Chicken with Cauliflower and Carrots
Day 18	Breakfast Taco Scramble	Salmon Pasta	Harissa Yogurt Chicken Thighs
Day 19	Cauliflower Fritters with Hummus	Skillet Fried Cod	Braised Chicken with Wild Mushrooms
Day 20	Overnight Berry Chia Oats	Slow-Cooked Kalua Pork and Cabbage	Braised Duck with Fennel Root
Day 21	Feta and Quinoa Egg Muffins	Steak Pinwheels	Chicken Gyros with Tzatziki
Day 22	5-Minute Heirloom Tomato and Cucumber Toast	Tangy Shrimp	Eggplant Casserole
Day 23	Garlic Parmesan Chicken Wings	Beef and Broccoli Roast	Dijon and Herb Pork Tenderloin
Day 24	Feta Avocado and Mashed Chickpea Toast	Fried green beans rosemary	Steak with Red Wine–Mushroom Sauce
Day 25	Pilaf with Cream Cheese	Crispy broccoli pop corn	Greek Meatballs
Day 26	Easy Spaghetti Squash	Cheesy cauliflower croquettes	Lamb with String Beans
Day 27	Creamy Mango and Banana Overnight Oats	Spinach in cheese envelopes	Fish Fillet on Lemons

Day 28	Bacon and Eggs with Tomatoes	Cheesy mushroom slices	Tilapia Fillet with Onion and Avocado
Day 29	Sun-Dried Tomatoes Oatmeal	Asparagus fries	Sea Bass Crusted with Moroccan Spices
Day 30	Breakfast Egg on Avocado	Kale chips	Classic Escabeche
Day 31	Potato Scallops with Truffle Oil	Guacamole	Thyme Whole Roasted Red Snapper
Day 32	Mediterranean Pasta with Basil	Zucchini noodles	Crispy Fried Sardines
Day 33	Brekky Egg-Potato Hash	Cauliflower soufflé	Fish and Orzo
Day 34	Cinnamon Porridge	Banana Waffles	Spiced Soup with Lentils and Legumes
Day 35	Cherry Smoothie Bowl	Turkey Burgers with Mango Salsa	Brown Rice Pilaf with Golden Raisins
Day 36	Bacon and Cream Cheese Mug Muffins	Grilled Pesto Salmon with Asparagus	Ritzy Veggie Chili
Day 37	Cinnamon and Pecan Porridge	Cheddar-Stuffed Burgers with Zucchini	Spicy Italian Bean Balls with Marinara
Day 38	Dinosaur Eggs	Chicken Cordon Bleu with Cauliflower	Baked Rolled Oat with Pears and Pecans
Day 39	Dill and Tomato Frittata	Rosemary Roasted Pork with Cauliflower	Greek Green Beans
Day 40	Paleo Almond Banana Pancakes	Chicken Tikka with Cauliflower Rice	Spicy Zucchini
Day 41	Zucchini with Egg	Beef and Broccoli Stir-Fry	Carrot Potato Medley

Day	Breakfast	Lunch	Dinner
Day 42	Cheesy Amish Breakfast Casserole	Parmesan-Crusted Halibut with Asparagus	Flavors Basil Lemon Ratatouille
Day 43	Breakfast Couscous	Hearty Beef and Bacon Casserole	Feta Green Beans
Day 44	Avocado and Apple Smoothie	Sesame Wings with Cauliflower	Delicious Pepper Zucchini
Day 45	Mini Frittatas	Baked Zucchini Noodles with Feta	Lemon Artichokes
Day 46	Italian Breakfast Sausage with Baby Potatoes and Vegetables	Brussels Sprouts With Bacon	Delicious Okra
Day 47	Blueberry Greek Yogurt Pancakes	Bun less Burger - Keto Style	Parsnips With Eggplant
Day 48	Pastry-Less Spanakopita	Coffee BBQ Pork Belly	Eggplant With Olives
Day 49	Date and Walnut Overnight Oats	Garlic and Thyme Lamb Chops	Zucchini Tomato Potato Ratatouille
Day 50	Pear and Mango Smoothie	Jamaican Jerk Pork Roast	Tomato Stuffed with Cheese and Peppers
Day 51	Greek Yogurt w/ Berries and Seeds	Mixed Vegetable Patties - Instant Pot	Loaded Portobello Mushrooms
Day 52	Mediterranean Breakfast Egg White Sandwich	Roasted Leg of Lamb	Sumac Chicken with Cauliflower and Carrots
Day 53	Breakfast Taco Scramble	Salmon Pasta	Harissa Yogurt Chicken Thighs
Day 54	Cauliflower Fritters with Hummus	Skillet Fried Cod	Braised Chicken with Wild Mushrooms
Day 55	Overnight Berry Chia Oats	Slow-Cooked Kalua Pork and Cabbage	Braised Duck with Fennel Root
Day 56	Feta and Quinoa Egg Muffins	Steak Pinwheels	Chicken Gyros with Tzatziki

Measurement of Conversion

CONVERSION CHART

Liquid Measure

8 ounces =	1 cup
2 cups =	1 pint
16 ounces =	1 pint
4 cups =	1 quart
1 gill =	1/2 cup or 1/4 pint
2 pints =	1 quart
4 quarts =	1 gallon
31.5 gal. =	1 barrel
3 tsp =	1 tbsp
2 tbsp =	1/8 cup or 1 fluid ounce
4 tbsp =	1/4 cup
8 tbsp =	1/2 cup
1 pinch =	1/8 tsp or less
1 tsp =	60 drops

Conversion of US Liquid Measure to Metric System

1 fluid oz. =	29.573 milliliters
1 cup =	230 milliliters
1 quart =	.94635 liters
1 gallon =	3.7854 liters
.033814 fluid ounce =	1 milliliter
3.3814 fluid ounces =	1 deciliter
33.814 fluid oz. or 1.0567 qt.=	1 liter

Dry Measure

2 pints =	1 quart
4 quarts =	1 gallon
8 quarts =	2 gallons or 1 peck
4 pecks =	8 gallons or 1 bushel
16 ounces =	1 pound
2000 lbs. =	1 ton

Conversion of US Weight and Mass Measure to Metric System

.0353 ounces =	1 gram
1/4 ounce =	7 grams
1 ounce =	28.35 grams
4 ounces =	113.4 grams
8 ounces =	226.8 grams
1 pound =	454 grams
2.2046 pounds =	1 kilogram
.98421 long ton or 1.1023 short tons =	1 metric ton

Linear Measure

12 inches =	1 foot
3 feet =	1 yard
5.5 yards =	1 rod
40 rods =	1 furlong
8 furlongs (5280 feet) =	1 mile
6080 feet =	1 nautical mile

Conversion of US Linear Measure to Metric System

1 inch =	2.54 centimeters
1 foot =	.3048 meters
1 yard =	.9144 meters
1 mile =	1609.3 meters or 1.6093 kilometers
.03937 in. =	1 millimeter
.3937 in.=	1 centimeter
3.937 in.=	1 decimeter
39.37 in.=	1 meter
3280.8 ft. or .62137 miles =	1 kilometer

To convert a Fahrenheit temperature to Centigrade, do the following:
a. Subtract 32   b. Multiply by 5   c. Divide by 9

To convert Centigrade to Fahrenheit, do the following:
a. Multiply by 9   b. Divide by 5   c. Add 32

CHAPTER 4

Breakfast recipes

1

Bacon and Cream Cheese Mug Muffins

NUTRITION: CALORIES: 511 G, FATS: 38 G, PROTEIN: 16 G

15'

15'

2

INGREDIENTS

- ¼ cup flaxseed meal
- 1 egg
- 2 tablespoons heavy cream
- 2 tablespoons pesto
- ¼ cup almond flour
- ¼ teaspoon baking soda
- Salt and black pepper to taste
- 2 tablespoons cream cheese
- 4 bacon slices
- ½ medium avocado, sliced

DIRECTIONS

1. Mix the flaxseed meal, almond flour, and baking soda in a bowl. Add the egg, heavy cream, and pesto. Then whisk well. Season with salt and pepper.
2. Divide the mixture between 2 ramekins. Microwave for 60–90 seconds. Let cool slightly before filling.
3. Put the bacon in a nonstick skillet and cook until crispy, then set aside.
4. Transfer the muffins onto a plate and cut them in half crosswise. Assemble the sandwiches by spreading the cream cheese and topping with the bacon and avocado slices.

2

Cinnamon and Pecan Porridge

NUTRITION: CALORIES: 580 G, FAT: 14 G, CARBS: 3 G, PROTEIN: 8 G

15'

10'

2

INGREDIENTS

- ½ teaspoon cinnamon
- ¼ cup pecans, chopped
- ¼ cup unsweetened coconut, toasted
- ¼ cup coconut milk
- ¼ cup almond butter
- ¾ cup unsweetened almond milk
- 1 tablespoon extra-virgin coconut oil
- 2 tablespoons hemp seeds
- 2 tablespoons whole chia seeds

DIRECTIONS

1. Place a small saucepan over medium heat. Combine the coconut milk, coconut oil, almond butter, and almond milk. Bring to simmer and remove from heat.
2. Add the toasted coconut (leave some for the topping), cinnamon, pecans, hemp seeds, and chia seeds. Mix the ingredients well and allow to rest for 5–10 minutes.
3. Divide between two bowls and serve.

3

Dinosaur Eggs

NUTRITION: CALORIES: 784, FAT: 63.2 G, CARBS: 34 G, PROTEIN: 19.9 G

20'

15'

4

INGREDIENTS

- Mustard sauce: ¼ cup coarse mustard, ¼ cup Greek yogurt
- 1 teaspoon garlic powder, 1 pinch of cayenne pepper
- Eggs: 2 beaten eggs 2 cups of mashed potato flakes 4 boiled eggs, peeled
- 1 can (15 oz) HORMEL® Mary Kitchen® minced beef finely chopped can
- 2 liters of vegetable oil for frying

DIRECTIONS

1. Combine the old-fashioned mustard, Greek yogurt, garlic powder, and cayenne pepper in a small bowl until smooth.
2. Place 2 beaten eggs in a shallow dish; place the potato flakes in a separate shallow dish.
3. Divide the minced meat into 4 Servings. Form salted beef around each egg until it is completely wrapped.
4. Roll the wrapped eggs in the beaten egg and brush with mashed potatoes until they are covered.
5. Heat the oil in a frying pan or large saucepan at 190°C (375°F).
6. Put 2 eggs in the hot oil and bake for 3 to 5 minutes until brown. Remove with a spoon and place on a plate lined with kitchen paper. Repeat this with the remaining 2 eggs.
7. Cut lengthwise and serve with a mustard sauce.

4

Dill and Tomato Frittata

NUTRITION: CALORIES: 149, PROTEIN: 13.26 G, CARBS: 9.93 G, FAT: 10.28 G

10'

35'

6

INGREDIENTS

- Pepper and salt to taste
- 1 teaspoon red pepper flakes
- 2 garlic cloves, minced
- ½ cup crumbled goat cheese (optional)
- 2 tablespoons fresh chives, chopped
- 2 tablespoons fresh dill, chopped
- 4 tomatoes, diced
- 8 eggs, whisked
- 1 teaspoon coconut oil

DIRECTIONS

1. Grease a 9-inch round baking pan and preheat the oven to 325°F.
2. In a large bowl, mix well all ingredients and pour into prepped pan.
3. Pop into the oven and bake until the middle is cooked through around 30–35 minutes.
4. Remove from oven and garnish with more chives and dill.

5

Paleo Almond Banana Pancakes

NUTRITION: CALORIES: 306, PROTEIN: 14.4 G, CARBS: 3.6 G, FAT: 26.0 G

10'

10'

3

INGREDIENTS

- ¼ cup almond flour
- ½ teaspoon ground cinnamon
- 3 eggs
- 1 banana, mashed
- 1 tablespoon almond butter
- 1 teaspoon vanilla extract
- 1 teaspoon olive oil
- Sliced banana to serve

DIRECTIONS

1. Whisk the eggs in a mixing bowl until they become fluffy.
2. In another bowl, mash the banana using a fork and add to the egg mixture.
3. Add the vanilla, almond butter, cinnamon and almond flour.
4. Mix into a smooth batter.
5. Heat the olive oil in a skillet.
6. Add one spoonful of the batter and fry them on both sides.
7. Keep doing these steps until you are done with all the batter.
8. Add some sliced banana on top before serving.

6

Zucchini with Egg

NUTRITION: CALORIES: 213, FAT: 15.7 G, CARBS: 11.2 G, PROTEIN: 10.2 G

5'

10'

2-4

INGREDIENTS

- 1 ½ tablespoon olive oil
- 2 large zucchinis, cut into large chunks
- Salt and ground black pepper to taste
- 2 large eggs
- 1 teaspoon water, or as desired

DIRECTIONS

1. Heat the oil in a frying pan over medium heat; sauté zucchini until soft, about 10 minutes.
2. Season the zucchini with salt and black pepper.
3. Beat the eggs with a fork in a bowl.
4. Add water and beat until everything is well mixed.
5. Pour the eggs over the zucchini; boil and stir until scrambled eggs and no more flowing, about 5 minutes. Season zucchini and eggs with salt and black pepper.

Cheesy Amish Breakfast Casserole

NUTRITION: CALORIES: 314, FAT: 22.8 G, CARBS: 12.1 G, PROTEIN: 21.7 G

10'

50'

12

INGREDIENTS
- 1-pound sliced bacon, diced
- 1 sweet onion
- 1 pound Minced meat
- 4 cups grated and frozen potatoes, thawed
- 9 lightly beaten eggs
- 2 cups grated cheddar cheese
- 1 ½ cup cottage cheese
- 1 ¼ cups grated Swiss cheese

DIRECTIONS
1. Preheat the oven to 175°C (350°F). Grease a 9x13-inch baking dish.
2. Heat a large frying pan over medium heat; cook and stir the bacon and onion until the bacon is evenly browned about 10 minutes. Drain.
3. Stir in potatoes, eggs, cheddar cheese, cottage cheese, and Swiss cheese. Pour the mixture into a prepared baking dish.
4. Bake in the preheated oven until the eggs are cooked and the cheese is melted for 45 to 50 minutes. Let stand for 10 minutes before cutting and serving.

Breakfast Couscous

NUTRITION: CALORIES: 306, FAT: 6 G, PROTEIN: 11 G

9'

5'

4

INGREDIENTS
- 3 cup low-fat milk
- 1 cup whole-wheat couscous, uncooked
- 1 cinnamon stick
- ½ apricot, chopped, dried
- ¼ cup currants, dried
- 6 teaspoons brown sugar
- ¼ teaspoon salt
- 4 teaspoons melted butter

DIRECTIONS
1. Take a large saucepan and combine the milk and cinnamon stick and heat over medium.
2. Heat for 3 minutes or until micro bubbles forms around the edges of the pan. Do not boil.
3. Remove from heat and stir in the couscous, apricots, currants, salt, and 4 teaspoons of brown sugar.
4. Wrap mixture and allow it to sit for 15 minutes. Remove and throw away the cinnamon stick.
5. Divide couscous among 4 bowls, and top each with 1 teaspoon melted butter and ½ teaspoon brown sugar. Ready to serve.

9

Avocado and Apple Smoothie

NUTRITION: CALORIES: 208, FAT: 10.1 G, PROTEIN: 2.1 G

INGREDIENTS

- 3 cup spinach
- 1 cored green apple, chopped
- 1 pitted avocado, peeled and chopped
- 3 tablespoons chia seeds
- 1 teaspoon honey
- 1 frozen banana, peeled
- 2 cups coconut water

DIRECTIONS

1. Using your blender, add all the ingredients.
2. Process well for 5 minutes to obtain a smooth consistency and serve in glasses.

10

Mini Frittatas

NUTRITION: CALORIES: 55, FAT: 3 G, PROTEIN: 4.2 G

INGREDIENTS

- 1 yellow onion, chopped
- 1 cup Parmesan cheese, grated
- 1 yellow bell pepper, chopped
- 1 red bell pepper, chopped
- 1 zucchini, chopped
- Salt and black pepper
- A drizzle of olive oil
- 8 whisked eggs
- 2 tablespoons chives, chopped

DIRECTIONS

1. Set a pan over medium-high heat. Add in oil to warm.
2. Stir in all ingredients except chives and eggs. Sauté for around 5 minutes. Put the eggs on a muffin pan and top with the chives.
3. Set oven to 350°F/176°C. Place the muffin pan into the oven to bake for about 10 minutes.
4. Serve the eggs on a plate with sautéed vegetables.

11

Italian Breakfast Sausage with Baby Potatoes and Vegetables

NUTRITION: CALORIES: 321, FAT: 16 G, CARBS: 23 G, PROTEIN: 22 G

15'

30'

4

INGREDIENTS
- 1 pound sweet Italian sausage links, sliced on the bias (diagonal)
- 2 cups baby potatoes, halved
- 2 cups broccoli florets
- 1 cup onions cut into 1-inch chunks
- 2 cups small mushrooms, half or quarter the large ones for uniform size
- 1 cup baby carrots
- 2 tablespoons olive oil
- ½ teaspoon garlic powder
- ½ teaspoon Italian seasoning
- 1 teaspoon salt
- ½ teaspoons pepper

DIRECTIONS
1. Preheat the oven to 400°F. In a large bowl, add the baby potatoes, broccoli florets, onions, small mushrooms, and baby carrots.
2. Add in the olive oil, salt, pepper, garlic powder, and Italian seasoning and toss to coat evenly. Spread the vegetables onto a sheet pan in one even layer.
3. Arrange the sausage slices on the pan over the vegetables. Bake for 30 minutes—make sure to sake halfway through to prevent sticking. Allow cooling.
4. Distribute the Italian sausages and vegetables among the containers and store them in the fridge for 2–3 days.

12

Blueberry Greek Yogurt Pancakes

NUTRITION: CALORIES: 258, CARBS: 33 G, FAT: 8 G, PROTEIN: 11 G

15'

15'

6

INGREDIENTS
- 1¼ cup all-purpose flour
- 2 teaspoons baking powder
- 1 teaspoon baking soda
- ¼ teaspoon salt
- ¼ cup sugar
- 3 eggs
- 3 tablespoons vegan butter unsalted, melted
- ½ cup milk
- 1 ½ cup Greek yogurt plain, non-fat
- ½ cup blueberries optional

Toppings:
- Greek yogurt
- Mixed berries: blueberries, raspberries and blackberries

DIRECTIONS
1. In a large bowl, whisk together the flour, salt, baking powder and baking soda.
2. In a separate bowl, whisk together butter, sugar, eggs, Greek yogurt, and milk until the mixture is smooth.
3. Then add in the Greek yogurt mixture from step to the dry mixture in step 1, mix to combine, and allow the batter to sit for 20 minutes to get a smooth texture—if using blueberries fold them into the pancake batter.
4. Heat the pancake griddle, spray with non-stick butter spray or just brush with butter. Pour the batter, in ¼ cupful, onto the griddle.
5. Cook until the bubbles on top burst and create small holes, lift up the corners of the pancake to see if they're golden brown on the bottom
6. With a wide spatula, flip the pancake and cook on the other side until lightly browned. Serve.

13

Pastry-Less Spanakopita

NUTRITION: CALORIES: 325, PROTEIN: 11.2 G, FAT: 27.9 G, CARBS: 7.3 G

5'

20'

4

INGREDIENTS

- ⅛ teaspoons black pepper, add as per taste
- ⅓ cup Extra-virgin olive oil
- 4 lightly beaten eggs
- 7 cups Lettuce, preferably a spring mix (mesclun)
- ½ cup crumbled Feta cheese
- ⅛ teaspoon Sea salt, add to taste
- 1 finely chopped medium yellow onion

DIRECTIONS

1. Warm the oven to 180°C and grease the flan dish.
2. Once done, pour the extra-virgin olive oil into a large saucepan and heat it over medium heat with the onions, until they are translucent.
3. Add greens and keep stirring until all the ingredients are wilted. Season it with salt and pepper and transfer the greens to the prepared dish and sprinkle on some feta cheese.
4. Pour the eggs and bake for 20 minutes till it is cooked through and slightly brown.

14

Date and Walnut Overnight Oats

NUTRITION: CALORIES: 350, PROTEIN: 14 G, FAT: 12 G, CARBS: 49 G

5'

20'

2

INGREDIENTS

- ¼ cup Greek yogurt, plain
- ⅓ cup yogurt
- ⅔ cup oats
- 1 cup milk
- 2 teaspoons date syrup or you can also use maple syrup or honey
- 1 mashed banana
- ¼ teaspoon cinnamon
- ¼ cup walnuts
- A pinch of salt (approx. ⅛ teaspoon)

DIRECTIONS

1. Firstly, get a mason jar or a small bowl and add all the ingredients.
2. After that stir and mix all the ingredients well. Cover it securely, and cool it in a refrigerator overnight.
3. After that, take it out the next morning, add more liquid or cinnamon if required, and serve cold. (However, you can also microwave it for people with a warmer palate.)

15

Pear and Mango Smoothie

NUTRITION: CALORIES: 293, FAT: 8 G, CARBS: 53 G, PROTEIN: 8 G

5'

0'

1

INGREDIENTS

- 1 ripe mango, cored and chopped
- ½ mango, peeled, pitted and chopped
- 1 cup kale, chopped
- ½ cup plain Greek yogurt
- 2 ice cubes

DIRECTIONS

1. Add pear, mango, yogurt, kale, and mango to a blender and puree.
2. Add ice and blend until you have a smooth texture.
3. Serve and enjoy!

16

Greek Yogurt with Berries and Seeds

NUTRITION: CALORIES: 127, PROTEIN: 2.28 G, FAT: 3.66 G, CARBS: 23.49 G

3'

0'

1

INGREDIENTS

- A handful of blueberries
- a handful of raspberries
- 1 tablespoon Greek yogurt
- 1 teaspoon sunflower seeds
- 1 teaspoon pumpkin seeds
- 1 teaspoon sliced almonds

DIRECTIONS

1. Wash and dry your berries. Place them into a dish.
2. Spoon your Greek yogurt on top and sprinkle it with your seeds and almonds.
3. Serve and enjoy!

Mediterranean Breakfast Egg White Sandwich

NUTRITION: CALORIES: 458, CARBS: 51 G, FAT: 0 G, PROTEIN: 21 G

15'

30'

1

INGREDIENTS

- 1 teaspoon vegan butter
- ¼ cup egg whites
- 1 teaspoon chopped fresh herbs such as parsley, basil, rosemary
- 1 whole-grain seeded ciabatta roll
- 1 tablespoon pesto
- 1 or 2 slices Muenster cheese (or other cheese such as provolone, Monterey jack, etc.)
- About ½ cup roasted tomatoes
- Salt to taste
- Pepper to taste

For the roasted tomatoes:

- 10 oz grape tomatoes
- 1 tablespoon extra-virgin olive oil
- Kosher salt to taste
- Coarse black pepper to taste

DIRECTIONS

1. In a small nonstick skillet over medium heat, melt the vegan butter.
2. Pour in egg whites, season with salt and pepper, sprinkle with fresh herbs, and cook for 3 to 4 minutes or until egg is done, flip once.
3. In the meantime, toast the ciabatta bread in the toaster. Once done, spread both halves with pesto.
4. Place the egg on the bottom half of the sandwich roll, folding, if necessary, top with cheese, add the roasted tomatoes, and top half of the rolled sandwich.
5. For the roasted tomatoes, preheat the oven to 400°F. Slice tomatoes in half lengthwise. Then place them onto a baking sheet and drizzle with the olive oil, toss to coat.
6. Season with salt and pepper and roast in the oven for about 20 minutes, until the skin appears wrinkled

Breakfast Taco Scramble

NUTRITION: CALORIES: 450, FAT: 19 G, CARBS: 24.5 G, PROTEIN: 46 G

15'

1h 25'

4

INGREDIENTS

- 8 large eggs, beaten
- ¼ teaspoon seasoning salt
- 1 pound 99% lean ground turkey
- 2 tablespoons Greek seasoning
- ½ small onion, minced
- 2 tablespoons bell pepper, minced
- 4 oz can tomato sauce
- ¼ cup water

For the potatoes:
- 12 (1 pound) baby gold or red potatoes, quartered
- 4 teaspoon olive oil
- ¾ teaspoon salt
- ½ teaspoon garlic powder
- Fresh black pepper to taste

DIRECTIONS

1. In a large bowl, beat the eggs, season with seasoning salt. Preheat the oven to 425°F. Spray a 9x12 or large oval casserole dish with cooking oil.
2. Add the potatoes, 1 tablespoon of oil, ¾ teaspoon salt, garlic powder and black pepper, and toss to coat. Bake for 45 minutes to 1 hour, tossing every 15 minutes.
3. In the meantime, brown the turkey in a large skillet over medium heat, breaking it up while it cooks. Once no longer pink, add in the Greek seasoning.
4. Add in the bell pepper, onion, tomato sauce, and water, stir and cover, simmer on low for about 20 minutes. Spray a different skillet with nonstick spray over medium heat.
5. Once heated, add in the eggs seasoned with ¼ teaspoon salt and scramble for 2 to 3 minutes, or cook until it sets.
6. Distribute ¾ cup turkey and ⅔ cup eggs and divide the potatoes in each storage container, store for 3 to 4 days.

Cauliflower Fritters with Hummus

NUTRITION: CALORIES: 333, CARBS: 45 G, FAT: 13 G, PROTEIN: 14 G

15'

15'

4

INGREDIENTS

- 2 (15 oz) cans chickpeas, divided
- 2 ½ tablespoon olive oil, divided, plus more for frying
- 1 cup onion, chopped, about ½ a small onion
- 2 tablespoons garlic, minced
- 2 cups cauliflower, cut into small pieces, about ½ a large head
- ½ teaspoon salt
- Black pepper

Topping:
- Hummus of choice
- Green onion, diced

DIRECTIONS

1. Preheat the oven to 400°F. Rinse and drain 1 can of the chickpeas, and place them on a paper towel to dry off well.
2. Then place the chickpeas into a large bowl, remove the loose skins that come off, and toss with 1 tablespoon of olive oil. Spread the chickpeas onto a large pan and sprinkle with salt and pepper.
3. Bake for 20 minutes, then stir and then bake an additional 5 to 10 minutes until very crispy.
4. Once the chickpeas are roasted, transfer them to a large food processor and process them until broken down and crumble. Don't over-process them and turn them into flour, as you need to have some texture. Place the mixture into a small bowl, and set aside.
5. In a large pan over medium-high heat, add the remaining 1 ½ tablespoon of olive oil. Once heated, add in the onion and garlic, cook until lightly golden brown, about 2 minutes.
6. Then add in the chopped cauliflower, cook for an additional 2 minutes until the cauliflower is golden.
7. Turn the heat down to low and cover the pan; cook until the cauliflower is fork-tender and the onions are golden brown and caramelized, often stirring about 3 to 5 minutes.
8. Transfer the cauliflower mixture to the food processor, drain and rinse the remaining can of chickpeas and add them into the food processor, along with the salt and a pinch of pepper.
9. Blend until smooth, and the mixture starts to ball. Stop to scrape down the sides as needed
10. Transfer the cauliflower mixture into a large bowl and add ¼ cup of the roasted chickpea crumbs. Stir until well combined.
11. In a large bowl over medium heat, add enough oil to lightly cover the bottom of a large pan. Working in batches, cook the patties until golden brown, about 2 to 3 minutes, flip and cook again. Serve.

Overnight Berry Chia Oats

NUTRITION: CALORIES: 405, CARBS: 65 G, FAT: 11 G, PROTEIN: 17 G

15'

5'

1

INGREDIENTS

- ½ cup Quaker oats rolled oats
- ¼ cup chia seeds
- 1 cup milk or water
- A pinch of salt and cinnamon
- Maple syrup or a different sweetener to taste
- 1 cup frozen berries of choice or smoothie leftovers

Toppings:
- Yogurt
- Berries

DIRECTIONS

1. In a jar with a lid, add the oats, seeds, milk, salt, and cinnamon and refrigerate overnight. On serving day, puree the berries in a blender.
2. Stir the oats, add in the berry puree and top with yogurt and more berries, nuts, honey, or garnish of your choice. Enjoy!

Feta and Quinoa Egg Muffins

NUTRITION: CALORIES: 295, CARBS: 3 G, FAT: 23 G, PROTEIN: 19 G

20'

45-50'

12

INGREDIENTS

- 1 cup cooked quinoa
- 2 cups baby spinach, chopped
- ½ cup kalamata olives
- 1 cup tomatoes
- ½ cup white onion
- 1 tablespoon fresh oregano
- ½ teaspoon salt
- 2 teaspoons + more for coating pans olive oil
- 8 eggs
- 1 cup crumbled feta cheese
- 12-cup muffin tin

DIRECTIONS

1. Heat the oven to reach 350°F. Lightly grease the muffin tray cups with a spritz of cooking oil.
2. Prepare a skillet using the medium temperature setting and add the oil. When it's hot, toss in the onions to sauté for 2 mins.
3. Dump the tomatoes into the skillet and sauté for one minute. Fold in the spinach and continue cooking until the leaves have wilted (1 min.).
4. Transfer the pot to the countertop and add the oregano and olives. Set it aside.
5. Crack the eggs into a mixing bowl, using an immersion stick blender to mix them thoroughly. Add the cooked veggies in with the rest of the fixings.
6. Stir until it's combined, and scoop the mixture into the greased muffin cups. Set the timer to bake the muffins for 30 minutes until browned, and the muffins are set. Cool for about ten minutes. Serve.

22

5-Minute Heirloom Tomato and Cucumber Toast

NUTRITION: CALORIES: 239, CARBS: 32 G, FAT: 11 G, PROTEIN: 7 G

10'

6-10'

1

INGREDIENTS

- 1 small heirloom tomato
- 1 Persian cucumber
- 1 teaspoon olive oil
- A pinch of oregano
- Kosher salt and pepper as desired
- 2 teaspoons low-fat whipped cream cheese
- 2 pieces Trader Joe's whole grain crispbread or your choice
- 1 teaspoon balsamic glaze

DIRECTIONS

1. Dice the cucumber and tomato.
2. Combine all the fixings except for the cream cheese.
3. Smear the cheese on the bread and add the mixture. Top it off with the balsamic glaze and serve.

23

Garlic Parmesan Chicken Wings

NUTRITION: CALORIES: 259, CARBS: 1.2 G, FAT: 20.3 G, PROTEIN: 17.5 G

10'

35'

4

INGREDIENTS

- 16 chicken wings, pasture-raised
- 2 teaspoons minced garlic
- 2 teaspoons minced parsley
- ¼ cup olive oil
- ¼ cup unsalted butter
- 1 cup grated parmesan cheese, full-fat
- 2 tablespoons chopped basil leaves

DIRECTIONS

1. Set oven to 450° F and let preheat.
2. In the meantime, place a large skillet pan over medium-high heat, add oil and when hot, add chicken wings.
3. Cook for 3 minutes per side until seared, and then transfer pan to heated oven.
4. Bake chicken wings for 20 to 30 minutes or until nicely golden brown and crispy.
5. When done, return the pan over medium heat, add garlic and butter and cook until butter melt completely and the chicken is well coated with the butter-garlic mixture.
6. Sprinkle cheese over chicken wings and remove the pan from heat.
7. Garnish with basil and serve.

24

Feta Avocado and Mashed Chickpea Toast

NUTRITION: CALORIES: 337, CARBS: 43 G, FAT: 13 G, PROTEIN: 13 G

10'

15'

4

INGREDIENTS
- 15 oz can chickpeas
- 2 oz (½ cup) diced feta cheese
- 1 pitted avocado
- 2 teaspoons lemon (or 1 tablespoon orange)
- ½ teaspoon black pepper
- 2 teaspoons honey
- 4 slices of multigrain toast

DIRECTIONS
1. Toast the bread. Drain the chickpeas in a colander. Scoop the avocado flesh into the bowl. Use a large fork/potato masher to mash them until the mix is spreadable.
2. Pour in the lemon juice, pepper, and feta. Combine and divide into the four slices of toast. Drizzle using the honey and serve.

25

Pilaf with Cream Cheese

NUTRITION: CALORIES: 364, PROTEIN: 5 G, FAT: 30 G, CARBS: 12 G

11'

34'

6

INGREDIENTS
- 2 cups yellow long grain rice, parboiled
- 1 cup onion
- 4 green onions
- 3 tablespoons butter
- 3 tablespoons vegetable broth
- 2 teaspoons cayenne pepper
- 1 teaspoon paprika
- ½ teaspoon cloves, minced
- 2 tablespoons mint leaves
- A bunch of fresh mint leaves to garnish
- 1 tablespoon olive oil

Cheese Cream:
- 3 tablespoons olive oil
- Sea salt and black pepper to taste
- 9 oz cream cheese

DIRECTIONS
1. Start by heating your oven to 360°F, and then get out a pan. Heat your butter and olive oil together, and cook your onions and spring onions for two minutes.
2. Add in your salt, pepper, paprika, cloves, vegetable broth, rice, and remaining seasoning.
3. Sauté for three minutes.
4. Wrap with foil, and bake for another half hour. Allow it to cool.
5. Mix in the cream cheese, cheese, olive oil, salt, and pepper. Serve your pilaf garnished with fresh mint leaves.

Easy Spaghetti Squash

NUTRITION: CALORIES: 423, PROTEIN: 18 G, FAT: 30 G, CARBS: 15 G

13'

45'

6

INGREDIENTS

- 2 spring onions, chopped fine
- 3 garlic cloves, minced
- 1 zucchini, diced
- 1 red bell pepper, diced
- 1 tablespoon Italian seasoning
- 1 tomato, small and chopped fine
- 1 tablespoon parsley, fresh and chopped
- A pinch of lemon pepper
- A dash of sea salt, fine
- 4 oz feta cheese, crumbled
- 3 Italian sausage links, casing removed
- 2 tablespoons olive oil
- 1 spaghetti sauce, halved lengthwise

DIRECTIONS

1. Prepare the oven to 350°F, and get out a large baking sheet. Coat it with cooking spray, and then put your squash on it with the cut side down.
2. Bake at 350°F for forty-five minutes. It should be tender.
3. Turn the squash over, and bake for five more minutes. Scrape the strands into a larger bowl.
4. Cook a tablespoon of olive oil in a skillet, and then add in your Italian sausage. Cook at eight minutes before removing it and placing it in a bowl.
5. Add another tablespoon of olive oil to the skillet and cook your garlic and onions until softened. This will take five minutes. Throw in your Italian seasoning, red peppers and zucchini. Cook for another five minutes. Your vegetables should be softened.
6. Mix in your feta cheese and squash, cooking until the cheese has melted.
7. Stir in your sausage, and then season with lemon pepper and salt. Serve with parsley and tomato.

27

Creamy Mango and Banana Overnight Oats

NUTRITION: CALORIES: 199, FAT: 8 G, CARBS: 9 G, PROTEIN: 4 G

10'

0'

1

INGREDIENTS

For the smoothie:
- 1 ripe banana
- ½ mango, peeled, cubed
- ½ tablespoon ground flaxseed
- 1 cup almond milk

For the oats:
- 1 cup oats
- 1 small ripe banana, mashed
- ½ cup almond milk
- ½ tablespoon ground flaxseed
- 2 tablespoons chia seeds
- Stevia or erythritol to taste

DIRECTIONS

1. Add all the smoothie ingredients into a blender and blend until smooth.
2. Pour into a tall glass.

To make the oats layer:

3. Add oats, almond milk, flaxseed, chia seeds, and stevia into a bowl. Stir well and add banana.
4. Mix until well combined. Pour it over the smoothie in the glass.
5. Chill in the refrigerator overnight and serve.

28

Bacon and Eggs with Tomatoes

NUTRITION: CALORIES: 110, FAT: 10 G, CARBS: 3 G, PROTEIN: 6 G

10'

30'

5

INGREDIENTS

- 4 large ripe tomatoes, halved
- 8 rashers smoked back bacon, trimmed of fat
- 4 eggs
- Salt to taste
- Pepper to taste
- 1 teaspoon vinegar

DIRECTIONS

1. Set up the grill to preheat. Let it preheat to high heat.
2. Place a rack on the grill pan. Line the pan with foil. Place tomatoes on the rack. Let it grill for 3 minutes. Place bacon along with the tomatoes.
3. Grill for 4 minutes until soft.
4. Meanwhile, place a large saucepan over medium-high heat. Fill the saucepan up to about ¾ with water. Let it boil.
5. When it begins to boil, add vinegar and stir. Crack an egg into a bowl and slowly slide the egg into the boiling water. Repeat this, one at a time.
6. Cook each egg until it is soft boiled, for 2-3 minutes.
7. Meanwhile, divide the bacon and tomatoes into 2 plates.
8. Remove the eggs with a slotted spoon and place them on the plates. Sprinkle salt and pepper and serve.

29

Sun-Dried Tomatoes Oatmeal

NUTRITION: CALORIES: 170, FAT: 17.8 G, PROTEIN: 1.5 G

4'

22'

INGREDIENTS

- 3 cup water
- 1 cup almond milk
- 1 tablespoon olive oil
- 1 cup steel-cut oats
- ¼ cup tomatoes, sun-dried, chopped
- A pinch of red pepper flakes

DIRECTIONS

1. Using a pan, add the water and milk to mix. Set on medium heat and allow to boil.
2. Set up another pan on medium-high heat. Warm the oil and add oats to cook for 2 minutes. Transfer to the first pan plus tomatoes then stir. Let simmer for approximately 20 minutes.
3. Set in serving bowls and top with red pepper flakes. Enjoy.

4

30

Breakfast Egg on Avocado

NUTRITION: CALORIES: 252, FAT: 20 G, PROTEIN: 14 G

9'

15'

INGREDIENTS

- 1 teaspoon garlic powder
- ½ teaspoon sea salt
- ¼ cup Parmesan cheese, shredded
- ¼ teaspoon black pepper
- 3 avocados, pitted, halved
- 6 eggs

DIRECTIONS

1. Prep muffin tins and preheat the oven to 350°F/176°C.
2. Split the avocado. To ensure that the egg would fit inside the cavity of the avocado, lightly scrape off ⅓ of the meat.
3. Place avocado on a muffin tin to ensure that it faces the top-up. Evenly season each avocado with pepper, salt, and garlic powder.
4. Add 1 egg to each avocado cavity and garnish the tops with cheese. Set in your oven to bake until the egg white is set, about 15 minutes. Serve and enjoy.

6

Potato Scallops with Truffle Oil

NUTRITION: CALORIES: 279, FAT: 59.8 G, PROTEIN: 24.5 G

8'

24'

1

INGREDIENTS

- 4 oz scallops
- 3 oz potato
- ½ oz Parmesan cheese
- ½ teaspoon lime zest
- ½ oz butter
- 1 tablespoon olive oil
- 1 ½ teaspoon truffle oil
- 1 teaspoon arugula
- ⅔ oz cherry tomatoes
- 1 chive
- ½ teaspoon thyme
- Sea salt to taste
- Ground black pepper to taste

DIRECTIONS

1. Fry the scallops on both sides in olive oil with thyme, salt, and pepper.
2. Separately, boil the potatoes and rub them through a sieve. Add the zest of lime, grated Parmesan cheese, butter, salt, and pepper.
3. Lightly warm the arugula and cherry tomatoes in olive oil.
4. Put the mashed potatoes through the ring on a plate, scallops symmetrically put on it, arugula and cherry on the scallops, garnish with the thyme and onion, and pour with the truffle oil.

Mediterranean Pasta with Basil

NUTRITION: CALORIES: 136, FAT: 3.2 G, PROTEIN: 4 G

12'

19'

4

INGREDIENTS

- 2 red bell peppers
- 2 red onions
- 2 chili peppers
- 3 garlic cloves
- 1 teaspoon brown sugar
- 2 tablespoons olive oil
- 2 pounds tomatoes
- ⅔ pound pasta
- 1 tablespoon fresh basil leaves
- 2 tablespoons Parmesan cheese, grated

DIRECTIONS

1. Preheat the oven to 390°F. Put the pepper, onion, chili, and garlic in a deep pan. Sprinkle with the sugar, drizzle with olive oil, and season with salt and ground black pepper to taste.
2. Bake in the oven for 15 minutes, add the chopped tomatoes and cook for another 15 minutes.
3. While the vegetables are baking, prepare the pasta following the instructions on the package.
4. Take out the vegetables from the oven and mix the pasta with them. Sprinkle top with parmesan and basil leaves.

33

Brekky Egg-Potato Hash

NUTRITION: CALORIES: 198, FAT: 0.7 G, PROTEIN: 4 G

8'

25'

2

INGREDIENTS

- 1 zucchini, diced
- ½ cup chicken broth
- ½ pound (220 g) cooked chicken
- 1 tablespoon olive oil
- 4 oz (113 g) shrimp
- Salt and black pepper
- 1 sweet potato, diced
- 2 eggs
- ¼ teaspoon cayenne pepper
- 2 teaspoons garlic powder
- 1 cup fresh spinach

DIRECTIONS

1. In a skillet, add olive oil.
2. Fry the shrimp, cooked chicken, and sweet potato for 2 minutes.
3. Add the cayenne pepper, garlic powder and toss for 4 minutes.
4. Add the zucchini and toss for another 3 minutes.
5. Whisk the eggs in a bowl and add to the skillet.
6. Season using salt and pepper. Cover with the lid.
7. Cook for 1 more minute and mix in the chicken broth.
8. Cover and cook for another 8 minutes on high heat.
9. Add the spinach, toss for 2 more minutes and serve.

34

Cinnamon Porridge

NUTRITION: CALORIES: 383, FAT: 14 G, CARBS: 3 G, PROTEIN: 8 G

10'

30'

4

INGREDIENTS

- 4 ½ oz jumbo porridge oats
- 20 oz semi-skimmed milk
- 1 teaspoon lemon juice
- ½ teaspoon ground cinnamon + extra to garnish
- 2 ripe medium pears, peeled, cored, grated

DIRECTIONS

1. Add oats, milk, and cinnamon into a nonstick saucepan. Place the saucepan over medium-low heat. Cook until creamy. Stir constantly.
2. Divide into bowls. Scatter pear on top. Drizzle lemon juice on top. Garnish with cinnamon and serve.

Cherry Smoothie Bowl

NUTRITION: CALORIES: 130, FATS: 0 G, PROTEIN: 1 G

15'

0'

1

INGREDIENTS

- ½ cup organic rolled oats
- ½ cup almond milk, unsweetened
- 1 tablespoon chia seeds
- 1 teaspoon hemp seeds
- 2 teaspoons almonds, sliced
- 1 tablespoon almond butter
- 1 teaspoon vanilla extract
- ½ cup berries, fresh
- 1 cup cherries, frozen
- 1 cup plain Greek yogurt

DIRECTIONS

1. Soak the organic rolled oats in almond milk.
2. Prepare a smooth blend with the soaked oats, frozen cherries, yogurt, chia seeds, almond butter, and vanilla extract. Pour the mixture into 2 bowls.
3. To each bowl, add equal parts of the hemp seeds, sliced almonds, and fresh cherries.

CHAPTER 5

Lunch Recipes

36

Grilled Pesto Salmon with Asparagus

NUTRITION: CALORIES: 300, FAT: 17.5 G, PROTEIN: 34.5 G, CARBS: 2.5 G

5'

15'

4

INGREDIENTS
- 4 (6-ounce) boneless salmon fillets
- Salt and pepper
- 1 bunch asparagus, ends trimmed
- 2 tablespoons olive oil
- ¼ cup basil pesto

DIRECTIONS
1. Preheat the grill to heat, and oil the grills.
2. Season the salmon with salt and pepper and sprinkle with spray to cook.
3. Grill the salmon on each side for 4 to 5 minutes, until cooked.
4. Throw the asparagus with oil and grill for about 10 minutes, until tender.
5. Spoon the salmon with the pesto, and serve with the asparagus.

37

Cheddar-Stuffed Burgers with Zucchini

NUTRITION: CALORIES: 440, FAT: 27.5 G, PROTEIN: 45 G, CARBS: 8 G

10'

15'

4

INGREDIENTS
- 1 pound ground beef (80% lean)
- 2 large eggs
- ¼ cup almond flour
- 1 cup shredded cheddar cheese
- Salt and pepper
- 2 tablespoons olive oil
- 1 large zucchini, halved and sliced

DIRECTIONS
1. In a cup, add the beef, egg, almond flour, cheese, salt, and pepper.
2. Mix well, then shape into 4 even-sized patties.
3. Heat up the oil over medium to high heat in a large skillet.
4. Add the burger patties, and cook until browned for 5 minutes.
5. Flip the patties onto the skillet and add the zucchini, tossing to cover with grease.
6. Add salt and pepper and boil for 5 minutes, stirring the mixture.

Chicken Cordon Bleu with Cauliflower

NUTRITION: CALORIES: 420, FAT: 23.5 G, PROTEIN: 45 G, CARBS: 7 G

10'

45'

4

INGREDIENTS

- 4 boneless chicken breast halves (about 12 oz)
- 4 slices deli ham
- 4 slices Swiss cheese
- 1 large egg, whisked well
- 2 oz pork rinds
- ¼ cup almond flour
- ¼ cup grated parmesan cheese
- ½ teaspoon garlic powder
- Salt and pepper
- 2 cups cauliflower florets

DIRECTIONS

1. Preheat the oven to 350°F and put a foil on a baking sheet.
2. Sandwich the breast half of the chicken between parchment parts and pound flat.
3. Spread the bits out and cover with ham and cheese sliced over.
4. Roll the chicken over the fillings and then dip it into the beaten egg.
5. In a food processor, mix the pork rinds, almond flour, parmesan, garlic powder, salt and pepper, and pulse into fine crumbs.
6. Roll the rolls of chicken in the mixture of pork rind then put them on the baking sheet.
7. Throw the cauliflower into the baking sheet with the melted butter and fold.
8. Bake for 45 minutes until the chicken is fully cooked.

Rosemary Roasted Pork with Cauliflower

NUTRITION: CALORIES: 300, FAT: 15.5 G, PROTEIN: 37 G, CARBS: 3 G

10'

20'

4

INGREDIENTS

- 1 ½ pound boneless pork tenderloin
- 1 tablespoon coconut oil
- 1 tablespoon fresh chopped rosemary
- Salt and pepper
- 1 tablespoon olive oil
- 2 cups cauliflower florets

DIRECTIONS

1. Rub the coconut oil into the pork, then season with the rosemary, salt, and pepper.
2. Heat up the olive oil over medium to high heat in a large skillet.
3. Put the pork on each side and cook until browned for 2 to 3 minutes.
4. Sprinkle the cauliflower over the pork in the skillet.
5. Reduce heat to low, then cover the skillet and cook until the pork is cooked through for 8 to 10 minutes.
6. Slice the pork with cauliflower and eat.

40

Chicken Tikka with Cauliflower Rice

NUTRITION: CALORIES: 485, FAT: 32 G, PROTEIN: 43 G, CARBS: 6.5 G

10'

6h

6

INGREDIENTS

- 2 pounds boneless chicken thighs, chopped
- 1 cup canned coconut milk
- 1 cup heavy cream
- 3 tablespoons tomato paste
- 2 tablespoons garam masala
- 1 tablespoon fresh grated ginger
- 1 tablespoon minced garlic
- 1 tablespoon smoked paprika
- 2 teaspoons onion powder
- 1 teaspoon guar gum
- 1 tablespoon butter
- 1 ½ cup rice cauliflower

DIRECTIONS

1. Place the chicken in a slow cooker and then stir in the remaining ingredients, except for the butter and cauliflower.
2. Cover and cook for 6 hours on low heat until the chicken is cooked and the sauce is thickened.
3. Melt the butter over medium to high heat into a saucepan.
4. Remove the riced cauliflower, and cook until tender for 6 to 8 minutes.
5. Serve cauliflower rice with chicken tikka.

41

Beef and Broccoli Stir-Fry

NUTRITION: CALORIES: 350, FAT: 19 G, PROTEIN: 37.5 G, CARBS: 6.5

20'

15'

4

INGREDIENTS

- ¼ cup soy sauce
- 1 tablespoon sesame oil
- 1 teaspoon garlic chili paste
- 1 pound beef sirloin
- 2 tablespoons almond flour
- 2 tablespoons coconut oil
- 2 cups chopped broccoli florets
- 1 tablespoon grated ginger
- 3 garlic cloves, minced

DIRECTIONS

1. In a small bowl, whisk the soy sauce, sesame oil, and chili paste together.
2. In a plastic freezer bag, slice the beef and mix with the almond flour.
3. Pour in the sauce and toss to coat for 20 minutes, then let rest.
4. Heat up the oil over medium to high heat in a large skillet.
5. In the pan, add the beef and sauce and cook until the beef is browned.
6. Move the beef to the skillet sides, and then add the broccoli, ginger, and garlic.
7. Sauté until tender-crisp broccoli, then throw it all together and serve hot.

Parmesan-Crusted Halibut with Asparagus

NUTRITION: CALORIES: 415, FAT: 26 G, PROTEIN: 42 G, CARBS: 6 G

INGREDIENTS

- 2 tablespoons olive oil
- ¼ cup butter, softened
- Salt and pepper
- ¼ cup grated Parmesan
- 1 pound asparagus, trimmed
- 2 tablespoons almond flour
- 4 (6-ounce) boneless halibut fillets
- 1 teaspoon garlic powder

DIRECTIONS

1. Preheat the oven to 400°F and line a foil-based baking sheet.
2. Throw the asparagus in olive oil and scatter it over the baking sheet.
3. In a blender, add the butter, Parmesan cheese, almond flour, garlic powder, salt and pepper, and mix until smooth.
4. Place the fillets with the asparagus on the baking sheet, and spoon the Parmesan over the eggs.
5. Bake for 10 to 12 minutes, and then broil until browned for 2 to 3 minutes.

10'
15'
4

Hearty Beef and Bacon Casserole

NUTRITION: CALORIES: 410, FAT: 25.5 G, PROTEIN: 37 G, CARBS: 7.5 G

INGREDIENTS

- 8 slices uncooked bacon
- 1 medium head cauliflower, chopped
- ¼ cup canned coconut milk
- Salt and pepper
- 2 pounds ground beef (80% lean)
- 8 oz mushrooms, sliced
- 1 large yellow onion, chopped
- 2 garlic cloves, minced

DIRECTIONS

1. Preheat to 375°F on the oven.
2. Cook the bacon in a skillet until it gets crispness, then drain and chop on paper towels.
3. Bring to boil a pot of salted water, and then add the cauliflower.
4. Boil until tender for 6 to 8 minutes then drain and add the coconut milk to a food processor.
5. Mix until smooth, then sprinkle with salt and pepper.
6. Cook the beef until browned in a pan, and then wash the fat away.
7. Remove the mushrooms, onion, and garlic, and then move to a baking platter.
8. Place on top of the cauliflower mixture and bake for 30 minutes.
9. Broil for 5 minutes on high heat, then sprinkle with bacon to serve.

25'
30'
8

44

Sesame Wings with Cauliflower

NUTRITION: CALORIES: 400, FAT: 28.5 G, PROTEIN: 31.5 G, CARBS: 4 G

5'

30'

4

INGREDIENTS

- 2 ½ tablespoons soy sauce
- 2 tablespoons sesame oil
- 1 ½ teaspoon balsamic vinegar
- 1 teaspoon minced garlic
- 1 teaspoon grated ginger
- Salt
- 1 pound chicken wing, the wings itself
- 2 cups cauliflower florets

DIRECTIONS

1. In a freezer bag, mix the soy sauce, sesame oil, balsamic vinegar, garlic, ginger, and salt, then add the chicken wings.
2. Coat flip, and then chill for 2 to 3 hours.
3. Preheat the oven to 400°F and line a foil-based baking sheet.
4. Spread the wings along with the cauliflower onto the baking sheet.
5. Bake for 35 minutes, and then sprinkle on to serve with sesame seeds.

45

Baked Zucchini Noodles with Feta

NUTRITION: CARBS: 5 G, PROTEIN: 4 G, FATS: 8 G, CALORIES: 105

15'

15'

1

INGREDIENTS

- 1 quartered plum tomato
- 2 spiralized zucchini
- 8 cubes feta cheese
- 1 teaspoon pepper
- 1 tablespoon olive oil

DIRECTIONS

1. Set the oven temperature to reach 375°F.
2. Slice the noodles with a spiralizer and put the olive oil, tomatoes, pepper, and salt.
3. Bake within 10 to 15 minutes. Transfer then put cheese cubes, toss. Serve.

46

Brussels Sprouts with Bacon

NUTRITION: CARBS: 3.9 G, PROTEIN: 7.9 G, FATS: 6.9 G, CALORIES: 113

15'

40'

6

INGREDIENTS
- 16 oz bacon
- 16 oz Brussels sprouts
- Black pepper

DIRECTIONS
1. Warm the oven to reach 400°F.
2. Slice the bacon into small lengthwise pieces. Put the sprouts and bacon with pepper.
3. Bake within 35 to 40 minutes. Serve.

47

Bun less Burger-Keto Style

NUTRITION: CARBS: 2 G, PROTEIN: 26 G, FATS: 40 G, CALORIES: 479

15'

25'

6

INGREDIENTS
- 1 pound ground beef
- 1 tablespoon Worcestershire sauce
- 1 tablespoon steak seasoning
- 2 tablespoons olive oil
- 4 oz onions

DIRECTIONS
1. Mix the beef, olive oil, Worcestershire sauce, and seasonings.
2. Grill the burger. Prepare the onions by adding one tablespoon of oil in a skillet to med-low heat. Sauté. Serve.

Coffee BBQ Pork Belly

NUTRITION: CARBS: 2.6 G, PROTEIN: 24 G, FATS: 68 G, CALORIES: 644

15'

60'

4

INGREDIENTS

- 1 ½ cup beef stock
- 2 pounds pork belly
- 4 tablespoons olive oil
- ¼ cup Low-carb barbecue dry rub
- 2 tablespoons Instant Espresso Powder

DIRECTIONS

1. Set the oven to 350°F.
2. Heat up the beef stock in a small saucepan.
3. Mix in the dry barbecue rub and espresso powder.
4. Put the pork belly, skin side up in a shallow dish, and drizzle half of the oil over the top.
5. Put the hot stock around the pork belly. Bake within 45 minutes.
6. Sear each slice within three minutes per side. Serve.

Garlic and Thyme Lamb Chops

NUTRITION: CARBS: 1 G, PROTEIN: 14 G, FATS: 21 G, CALORIES: 252

15'

10'

6

INGREDIENTS

- 6–4 oz lamb chops
- 4 whole garlic cloves
- 2 thyme sprigs
- 1 teaspoon ground thyme
- 3 tablespoons olive oil

DIRECTIONS

1. Warm up a skillet. Put the olive oil. Rub the chops with the spices.
2. Put the chops in the skillet with the garlic and sprigs of thyme.
3. Sauté within 3 to 4 minutes and serve.

50

Jamaican Jerk Pork Roast

NUTRITION: CARBS: 0 G, PROTEIN: 23 G, FATS: 20 G, CALORIES: 282

15'

4h

12

INGREDIENTS

- 1 tablespoon olive oil
- 4 pounds pork shoulder
- ½ cup beef broth
- ¼ cup Jamaican Jerk spice blend

DIRECTIONS

1. Rub the roast well with the oil and the jerk spice blend. Sear the roast on all sides. Put the beef broth.
2. Simmer within four hours on low. Shred and serve.

51

Mixed Vegetable Patties-Instant Pot

NUTRITION: CARBS: 3 G, PROTEIN: 4 G, FATS: 10 G, CALORIES: 220

15'

10'

4

INGREDIENTS

- 1 cup cauliflower florets
- 1 bag of vegetables
- 1 ½ cup water
- 1 cup flax meal
- 2 tablespoon olive oil

DIRECTIONS

1. Steam the veggies to the steamer basket within 4 to 5 minutes. Mash in the flax meal.
2. Shape into 4 patties. Cook the patties within 3 minutes per side. Serve.

52

Roasted Leg of Lamb

NUTRITION: CARBS: 1 G, PROTEIN: 22 G, FATS: 14 G, CALORIES: 223

15'

1h 30'

6

INGREDIENTS

- ½ cup reduced-sodium beef broth
- 2 pounds lamb leg
- 6 garlic cloves
- 1 tablespoon rosemary leaves
- 1 teaspoon black pepper

DIRECTIONS

1. Warm up the oven temperature to 400°F.
2. Put the lamb in the pan and put the broth and seasonings.
3. Roast for 30 minutes and lower the heat to 350°F. Cook within one hour.
4. Cool and serve.

53

Salmon Pasta

NUTRITION: CARBS: 3 G, PROTEIN: 21 G, FATS: 42 G, CALORIES: 470

15'

1h 30'

2

INGREDIENTS

- 2 tablespoons coconut oil
- 2 zucchinis
- 8 oz smoked salmon
- ¼ cup keto-friendly mayo

DIRECTIONS

1. Make noodle-like strands from the zucchini.
2. Warm up the oil, put the salmon and sauté within 2 to 3 minutes.
3. Stir in the noodles and sauté for 1 to 2 more minutes.
4. Stir in the mayo and serve.

Skillet Fried Cod

NUTRITION: CARBS: 1 G, PROTEIN: 21 G, FATS: 7 G, CALORIES: 160

15'

30'

4

INGREDIENTS
- 6 garlic cloves
- 3 tablespoons ghee
- 4 cod fillets
- optional: garlic powder

DIRECTIONS
1. Toss half of the garlic into a skillet with the ghee.
2. Put the fillets in the pan, garlic, pepper and salt.
3. Turn it over, and add the remainder of the minced garlic. Cook.
4. Serve with garlic.

Slow-Cooked Kalua Pork and Cabbage

NUTRITION: CARBS: 4 G, PROTEIN: 22 G, TOTAL FATS: 13 G, CALORIES: 227

15'

11h

12

INGREDIENTS
- 3 pounds pork shoulder butt
- 1 medium cabbage
- 7 strips bacon
- 1 tablespoon coarse sea salt

DIRECTIONS
1. Trim the fat from the roast.
2. Layer most of the bacon in the cooker. Put salt over the roast and add to the slow cooker on top of the bacon. Cook on low within eight to ten hours. Put in the cabbage, and cook within an hour.
3. Shred the roast. Serve with cabbage and slow cooker juice.

56

Steak Pinwheels

NUTRITION: CARBS: 2 G, PROTEIN: 55 G, FATS: 20 G, CALORIES: 414

15'

25'

6

INGREDIENTS

- 2 pounds flank steak
- 8 oz pkg. mozzarella cheese
- 1 bunch spinach

DIRECTIONS

1. Warm up the oven to reach 350°F.
2. Slice the steak into six portions. Beat until thin with a mallet.
3. Shred the cheese using a food processor and sprinkle on the steak. Roll it up and tie it with cooking twine.
4. Line the pan with the pinwheels and place it on a layer of spinach. Bake within 25 minutes.

57

Tangy Shrimp

NUTRITION: CARBS: 3 G, PROTEIN: 23 G, FATS: 27 G, CALORIES: 335

15'

15'

2

INGREDIENTS

- 3 garlic
- ¼ cup olive oil
- ½ pound jumbo shrimp
- 1 lemon
- Cayenne pepper

DIRECTIONS

1. Sauté the garlic and cayenne with the olive oil. Peel and devein the shrimp.
2. Cook within 2 to 3 minutes per side. Put pepper, salt, and lemon wedges.
3. Use the rest of the garlic oil for a dipping sauce. Serve.

Beef and Broccoli Roast

NUTRITION: CALORIES: 803, CARBS: 18 G, PROTEIN: 74 G, FATS: 49 G

15'

4h 30'

INGREDIENTS
- 1 pound beef chuck roast
- ½ cup beef broth
- ¼ cup Soy sauce
- 1 teaspoon toasted sesame oil
- 1 (16-ounce) bag frozen broccoli

DIRECTIONS
1. With the crock insert in place, preheat your slow cooker to low. On a cutting board, season the chuck roast with pink salt and pepper, and slice the roast thin.
2. Put the sliced beef in your slow cooker. Combine sesame oil and beef broth in a small bowl then pour over the beef.
3. Cover and cook on low for 4 hours. Add the frozen broccoli and cook for 30 minutes more. If you need more liquid, add additional beef broth. Serve hot.

2

Fried Green Beans Rosemary

NUTRITION: CALORIES: 72, FAT: 6.3 G, PROTEIN: 0.7 G, CARBS: 4.5 G

10'

5'

INGREDIENTS
- ¾ cup green beans
- 3 teaspoons minced garlic
- 2 tablespoons rosemary
- ½ teaspoon salt
- 1 tablespoon butter

DIRECTIONS
1. Warm up an air fryer to 390°F.
2. Put the chopped green beans then brush with butter. Sprinkle salt, minced garlic, and rosemary over then cook within 5 minutes. Serve.

2

60

Crispy Broccoli Pop Corn

NUTRITION: CALORIES: 202, FAT: 17.5 G, PROTEIN: 5.1 G, CARBS: 7.8 G

15'

10'

4

INGREDIENTS

- 2 cups broccoli florets
- 2 cups coconut flour
- 4 egg yolks
- ½ teaspoon salt
- ½ teaspoon pepper
- ¼ cup butter

DIRECTIONS

1. Dissolve butter, and then let it cool. Break the eggs in it.
2. Put coconut flour into the liquid, then put salt and pepper. Mix.
3. Warm up an air fryer to 400°F.
4. Dip a broccoli floret in the coconut flour mixture, and then place it in the air fryer.
5. Cook the broccoli florets for 6 minutes. Serve.

61

Cheesy Cauliflower Croquettes

NUTRITION: CALORIES: 160, FAT: 13 G, PROTEIN: 6.8 G, CARBS: 5.1 G

10'

16'

4

INGREDIENTS

- 2 cups cauliflower florets
- 2 teaspoons garlic
- ½ cup onion
- ¾ teaspoon mustard
- ½ teaspoon salt
- ½ teaspoon pepper
- 2 tablespoons butter
- ¾ cup cheddar cheese

DIRECTIONS

1. Microwave the butter. Let it cool.
2. Process the cauliflower florets using a processor. Transfer to a bowl then put chopped onion and cheese.
3. Put minced garlic, mustard, salt, and pepper, then pour melted butter over. Shape the cauliflower batter into medium balls.
4. Warm up an air fryer to 400°F and cook within 14 minutes. Serve.

Spinach in Cheese Envelopes

NUTRITION: CALORIES: 365, FAT: 34.6 G, PROTEIN: 10.4 G, CARBS: 4.4 G

15'

30'

INGREDIENTS

- 3 cups cream cheese
- 1½ cup coconut flour
- 3 egg yolks
- 2 eggs
- ½ cup cheddar cheese
- 2 cups steamed spinach
- ¼ teaspoon salt
- ½ teaspoon pepper
- ¼ cup onion

DIRECTIONS

1. Whisk cream cheese and put egg yolks. Stir in coconut flour until becoming soft dough.
2. Put the dough on a flat surface then roll until thin. Cut the thin dough into 8 squares.
3. Beat the eggs, and then place them in a bowl. Put salt, pepper, and grated cheese.
4. Put chopped spinach and onion into the egg batter.
5. Put spinach filling on a square dough then fold until becoming an envelope. Glue with water.
6. Warm up an air fryer to 425°F (218°C). Cook within 12 minutes.
7. Remove and serve!

Cheesy Mushroom Slices

NUTRITION: CALORIES: 365, FAT: 34.6 G, PROTEIN: 10.4 G, CARBS: 4.4 G

8-10'

15'

8

INGREDIENTS

- 2 cups mushrooms
- 2 eggs
- ¾ cup almond flour
- ½ cup cheddar cheese
- 2 tablespoons butter
- ½ teaspoon pepper
- ¼ teaspoon salt

DIRECTIONS

1. Processes chopped mushrooms in a food processor then add eggs, almond flour, and cheddar cheese.
2. Put salt and pepper then pour melted butter into the food processor. Transfer.
3. Warm up an air fryer to 375°F (191°C).
4. Put the loaf pan on the air fryer's rack then cook within 15 minutes. Slice and serve.

64

Asparagus Fries

NUTRITION: CALORIES: 453, FAT: 33.4 G, PROTEIN: 19.1 G, CARBS: 5.5 G

10'

10'

4

INGREDIENTS

- 10 organic asparagus spears
- 1 tablespoon organic roasted red pepper
- ¼ cup almond flour
- ½ teaspoon garlic powder
- ½ teaspoon smoked paprika
- 2 tablespoons parsley
- ½ cup parmesan cheese, and full-fat
- 2 organic eggs
- 3 tablespoons mayonnaise, full-fat

DIRECTIONS

1. Warm up the oven to 425°F.
2. Process cheese in a food processor, add garlic and parsley and pulse for 1 minute.
3. Add almond flour, pulse for 30 seconds, transfer and put paprika.
4. Whisk eggs into a shallow dish.
5. Dip asparagus spears into the egg batter, then coat with parmesan mixture and place it on a baking sheet. Bake in the oven within 10 minutes.
6. Put the mayonnaise in a bowl; add red pepper and whisk, and then chill. Serve with prepared dip.

65

Kale Chips

NUTRITION: CALORIES: 163, FAT: 10 G, PROTEIN: 2 G, CARBS: 14 G

5'

12'

4

INGREDIENTS

- 1 organic kale
- 1 tablespoon seasoned salt
- 2 tablespoons olive oil

DIRECTIONS

1. Warm up the oven to 350°F.
2. Put kale leaves into a large plastic bag and add oil. Shake and then spread on a large baking sheet.
3. Bake within 12 minutes. Serve with salt.

66

Guacamole

NUTRITION: CALORIES: 16.5, FAT: 1.4 G, PROTEIN: 0.23 G, CARBS: 0.5 G

10'

0'

4

INGREDIENTS
- 2 organic avocados pitted
- ⅓ organic red onion
- 1 organic jalapeño
- ½ teaspoon salt
- ½ teaspoon ground pepper
- 2 tablespoons tomato salsa
- 1 tablespoon lime juice
- ½ organic cilantro

DIRECTIONS
1. Slice the avocado flesh horizontally and vertically.
2. Mix in onion, jalapeño, and lime juice in a bowl.
3. Put salt and black pepper, add salsa and mix. Fold in cilantro and serve.

67

Zucchini Noodles

NUTRITION: CALORIES: 298, FAT: 26.1 G, PROTEIN: 5 G, CARBS: 2.3 G

5'

6'

2

INGREDIENTS
- 2 zucchinis, spiralized into noodles
- 2 tablespoons butter, unsalted
- 1 ½ tablespoon garlic
- ¾ cup parmesan cheese
- ½ teaspoon sea salt
- ¼ teaspoon ground black pepper
- ¼ teaspoon red chili flakes

DIRECTIONS
1. Sauté butter and garlic within 1 minute.
2. Put zucchini noodles, cook within 5 minutes, then put salt and black pepper.
3. Transfer then top with cheese and sprinkle with red chili flakes. Serve.

Cauliflower Souffle

NUTRITION: CALORIES: 342, FAT: 28 G, PROTEIN: 17 G, CARBS: 5 G

10'

12'

6

INGREDIENTS

- 1 cauliflower, florets
- 2 eggs
- 2 tablespoons heavy cream
- 2 oz cream cheese
- ½ cup sour cream
- ½ cup asiago cheese
- 1 cup cheddar cheese
- ¼ cup chives
- 2 tablespoons butter, unsalted
- 6 bacon, sugar-free
- 1 cup water

DIRECTIONS

1. Pulse eggs, heavy cream, sour cream, cream cheese, and cheeses in a food processor.
2. Put cauliflower florets, pulse for 2 seconds, and then add butter and chives and pulse for another 2 seconds.
3. Put water in a pot, and insert a trivet stand.
4. Put the cauliflower batter in a greased round casserole dish then put the dish on the trivet stand.
5. Cook within 12 minutes at high. Remove, top with bacon, and serve.

Banana Waffles

NUTRITION: CARBS: 4 G, FAT: 13 G, PROTEIN: 5 G, CALORIES: 155

30'

30'

4

INGREDIENTS

- 4 eggs
- 1 ripe banana
- ¾ cup coconut milk
- ¾ cup almond flour
- 1 pinch of salt
- 1 tablespoon ground psyllium husk powder
- ½ teaspoon vanilla extract
- 1 teaspoon baking powder
- 1 teaspoon ground cinnamon
- Butter or coconut oil for frying

DIRECTIONS

1. Mash the banana thoroughly until you get a mashed potato consistency.
2. Add all the other ingredients in and whisk thoroughly and distribute evenly the dry and wet ingredients. You should be able to get a pancake-like consistency
3. Fry the waffles in a pan or use a waffle maker.
4. You can serve it with hazelnut spread and fresh berries. Enjoy!

Turkey Burgers with Mango Salsa

NUTRITION: CALORIES: 384, PROTEIN: 3 G, FAT: 16 G

15'

10'

6

INGREDIENTS

- 1 ½ pound ground turkey breast
- 1 teaspoon sea salt, divided
- ¼ teaspoon freshly ground black pepper
- 2 tablespoons extra-virgin olive oil
- 2 mangos, peeled, pitted, and cubed
- ½ red onion, finely chopped
- 1 lime juice
- 1 garlic clove, minced
- ½ jalapeño pepper, seeded and finely minced
- 2 tablespoons fresh cilantro leaves, chopped

DIRECTIONS

1. Form the turkey breast into 4 patties and season with ½ teaspoon of sea salt and pepper.
2. In a nonstick skillet over medium-high heat, heat the olive oil until it shimmers.
3. Add the turkey patties and cook for 5 minutes per side until browned.
4. While the patties cook, mix the mango, red onion, lime juice, garlic, jalapeño, cilantro, and remaining ½ teaspoon of sea salt in a small bowl. Spoon the salsa over the turkey patties and serve.

CHAPTER 6

Dinner recipes

Ritzy Veggie Chili

NUTRITION: CALORIES: 633, FAT: 16.3 G, PROTEIN: 31.7 G, CARBS: 97.0 G

15'

5h

4

INGREDIENTS

- 1 (28 oz/794-g) can chopped tomatoes, with the juice
- 1 (15 oz/425-g) can black beans, drained and rinsed
- 1 (15 oz/425-g) can redly beans, drained and rinsed
- 1 medium green bell pepper, chopped
- 1 yellow onion, chopped
- 1 tablespoon onion powder
- 1 teaspoon paprika
- 1 teaspoon cayenne pepper
- 1 teaspoon garlic powder
- ½ teaspoon sea salt
- ½ teaspoon ground black pepper
- 1 tablespoon olive oil
- 1 large Hass avocado, pitted, peeled, and chopped, for garnish

DIRECTIONS

1. Combine all the ingredients, except for the avocado, in the slow cooker. Stir to mix well.
2. Put the slow cooker lid on and cook on high for 5 hours or until the vegetables are tender and the mixture has a thick consistency.
3. Pour the chili into a large serving bowl. Allow to cool for 30 minutes, then spread with chopped avocado and serve.

Spicy Italian Bean Balls with Marinara

NUTRITION: CALORIES: 351, FAT: 16.4 G, PROTEIN: 11.5 G, CARBS: 42.9 G

15'

30'

2-4

INGREDIENTS

Bean Balls:
- 1 tablespoon extra-virgin olive oil
- ½ yellow onion, minced
- 1 teaspoon fennel seeds
- 2 teaspoons dried oregano
- ½ teaspoon crushed red pepper flakes
- 1 teaspoon garlic powder
- 1 (15 oz/425-g) can white beans (cannellini or navy), drained and rinsed
- ½ cup whole-grain bread crumbs
- Sea salt and ground black pepper to taste

Marinara:
- 1 tablespoon extra-virgin olive oil
- 3 garlic cloves, minced
- Handful basil leaves
- 1 (28 oz/794-g) can chop tomatoes with juice reserved
- Sea salt to taste

DIRECTIONS

1. Preheat the oven to 350°F (180°C). Line a baking sheet with parchment paper. Heat the olive oil in a nonstick skillet over medium heat until shimmering.
2. Add the onion and sauté for 5 minutes or until translucent. Sprinkle with fennel seeds, oregano, red pepper flakes, and garlic powder, then cook for 1 minute or until aromatic.
3. Pour the sautéed mixture into a food processor and add the beans and bread crumbs. Sprinkle with salt and ground black pepper, then pulse to combine well and the mixture holds together.
4. Shape the mixture into balls with a 2-ounce (57 g.) cookie scoop, then arrange the balls on the baking sheet.
5. Bake in the preheated oven for 30 minutes or until lightly browned. Flip the balls halfway through the cooking time.
6. While baking the beanballs, heat the olive oil in a saucepan over medium-high heat until shimmering. Add the garlic and basil and sauté for 2 minutes or until fragrant.
7. Fold in the tomatoes and juice. Bring to a boil. Reduce the heat to low. Put the lid on and simmer for 15 minutes. Sprinkle with salt.
8. Transfer the beanballs to a large plate and baste with marinara before serving.

Baked Rolled Oat with Pears and Pecans

NUTRITION: CALORIES: 479, FAT: 34.9 G, PROTEIN: 8.8 G, CARBS: 50.1 G

15'

30'

6

INGREDIENTS

- 2 tablespoons coconut oil, melted, plus more for greasing the pan
- 3 ripe pears, cored and diced
- 2 cups unsweetened almond milk
- 1 tablespoon pure vanilla extract
- ¼ cup pure maple syrup
- 2 cups gluten-free rolled oats
- ½ cup raisins
- ¾ cup chopped pecans
- ¼ teaspoon ground nutmeg
- 1 teaspoon ground cinnamon
- ½ teaspoon ground ginger
- ¼ teaspoon sea salt

DIRECTIONS

1. Preheat the oven to 350°F (180°C). Grease a baking dish with melted coconut oil, then spread the pears in a single layer on the baking dish evenly.
2. Combine the almond milk, vanilla extract, maple syrup, and coconut oil in a bowl. Stir to mix well.
3. Combine the remaining ingredients in a separate large bowl. Stir to mix well. Fold the almond milk mixture in the bowl, then pour the mixture over the pears.
4. Place the baking dish in the preheated oven and bake for 30 minutes or until lightly browned and set. Serve immediately.

Greek Green Beans

NUTRITION: CALORIES: 381, FAT: 25.8 G, CARBS: 37.7 G, PROTEIN: 6.6 G

10'

15'

4

INGREDIENTS

- 1 pound green beans, remove stems
- 2 potatoes, quartered
- 1 ½ onion, sliced
- 1 teaspoon dried oregano
- ¼ cup dill, chopped
- ¼ cup fresh parsley, chopped
- 1 zucchini, quartered
- ½ cup olive oil
- 1 cup water
- 14.5 oz can tomato, diced
- Salt and Black pepper to taste

DIRECTIONS

1. Add all ingredients into the inner pot of instant pot and stir everything well. Seal pot with lid and cook on high for 15 minutes.
2. Once done, release pressure using quick release. Remove lid. Stir well and serve.

75

Spicy Zucchini

NUTRITION: CALORIES: 69, FAT: 4.1 G, CARBS: 7.9 G, PROTEIN: 2.7 G

10'

5'

4

INGREDIENTS

- 4 zucchinis, cut into ½-inch pieces
- 1 cup of water
- ½ teaspoon Italian seasoning
- ½ teaspoon red pepper flakes
- 1 teaspoon garlic, minced
- 1 tablespoon olive oil
- ½ cup can tomato, crushed
- Salt

DIRECTIONS

1. Add water and zucchini into the instant pot. Seal pot with lid and cook on high for 2 minutes. Once done, release pressure using quick release. Remove lid.
2. Drain zucchini well and clean the instant pot.
3. Add oil into the inner pot of instant pot and set the pot on sauté mode.
4. Add garlic and sauté for 30 seconds.
5. Add remaining ingredients and stir well and cook for 2-3 minutes. Serve and enjoy.

76

Carrot Potato Medley

NUTRITION: CALORIES: 283, FAT: 5.6 G, CARBS: 51.3 G, PROTEIN: 10.2 G

10'

15'

6

INGREDIENTS

- 4 pounds of baby potatoes, clean and cut in half
- 1 ½ pound carrots, cut into chunks
- 1 teaspoon Italian seasoning
- 1 ½ cups vegetable broth
- 1 tablespoon garlic, chopped
- 1 onion, chopped
- 2 tablespoons olive oil
- Salt and Black pepper to taste

DIRECTIONS

1. Add oil into the inner pot of instant pot and set the pot on sauté mode.
2. Add onion and sauté for 5 minutes. Add carrots and cook for 5 minutes.
3. Add remaining ingredients and stir well. Seal pot with lid and cook on high for 5 minutes.
4. Once done, allow to release pressure naturally for 10 minutes then release the remaining using quick release. Remove lid. Stir and serve.

Flavors Basil Lemon Ratatouille

NUTRITION: CALORIES: 103, FAT: 6.8 G, CARBS: 10.6 G, PROTEIN: 2.4 G

10'

10'

8

INGREDIENTS

- 1 small eggplant, cut into cubes
- 1 cup fresh basil
- 2 cups grape tomatoes
- 1 onion, chopped
- 2 summer squash, sliced
- 2 zucchinis, sliced
- 2 tablespoons vinegar
- 2 tablespoons tomato paste
- 1 tablespoon garlic, minced
- 1 fresh lemon juice
- ¼ cup olive oil
- Salt to taste

DIRECTIONS

1. Add basil, vinegar, tomato paste, garlic, lemon juice, oil, and salt into the blender and blend until smooth.
2. Add eggplant, tomatoes, onion, squash, and zucchini into the instant pot.
3. Pour blended basil mixture over vegetables and stir well. Seal pot with lid and cook on high for 10 minutes.
4. Once done, allow to release pressure naturally. Remove lid. Stir well and serve.

Feta Green Beans

NUTRITION: CALORIES: 234, FAT: 6.1 G, CARBS: 40.7 G, PROTEIN: 9.7 G

10'

15'

4

INGREDIENTS

- 1 ½ pound of green beans, trimmed
- ¼ cup feta cheese, crumbled
- 28 oz can tomato, crushed
- 2 teaspoons oregano
- 1 teaspoon cumin
- ½ cup water
- 1 tablespoon olive oil
- 1 tablespoon garlic, minced
- 1 onion, chopped
- 1 pound of baby potatoes, clean and cut into chunks
- Salt and Black pepper to taste

DIRECTIONS

1. Add oil into the inner pot of instant pot and set the pot on sauté mode.
2. Add onion and garlic and sauté for 3-5 minutes.
3. Add remaining ingredients except for feta cheese and stir well. Seal pot with lid and cook on high for 10 minutes.
4. Once done, allow to release pressure naturally for 5 minutes then release the remaining using quick release. Remove lid. Top with feta cheese and serve.

Delicious Pepper Zucchini

NUTRITION: CALORIES: 42, FAT: 2.9 G, CARBS: 4 G, PROTEIN: 1 G

10'

10'

6

INGREDIENTS
- 1 zucchini, sliced
- 2 poblano peppers, sliced
- 1 tablespoon sour cream
- ½ teaspoon ground cumin
- 1 yellow squash, sliced
- 1 tablespoon garlic, minced
- ½ onion, sliced
- 1 tablespoon olive oil
- Salt to taste

DIRECTIONS
1. Add oil into the inner pot of instant pot and set the pot on sauté mode.
2. Add poblano peppers and sauté for 5 minutes.
3. Add onion and garlic and sauté for 3 minutes.
4. Add remaining ingredients except for sour cream and stir well. Seal pot with lid and cook on high for 2 minutes.
5. Once done, release pressure using quick release. Remove lid.
6. Add sour cream and stir well and serve.

Lemon Artichokes

NUTRITION: CALORIES: 83, FAT: 0.4 G, CARBS: 17.9 G, PROTEIN: 5.6 G

10'

20'

4

INGREDIENTS
- 4 artichokes, trim and cut the top
- ¼ cup fresh lemon juice
- 2 cups vegetable stock
- 1 teaspoon lemon zest, grated
- Salt and Black pepper to taste

DIRECTIONS
1. Pour the stock into the instant pot then place the steamer rack in the pot.
2. Place artichoke steam side down on the steamer rack into the pot.
3. Sprinkle lemon zest over artichokes. Season with pepper and salt.
4. Pour lemon juice over artichokes. Seal pot with lid and cook on high for 20 minutes.
5. Once done, allow to release pressure naturally for 5 minutes then release the remaining using quick release. Remove lid. Serve and enjoy.

Delicious Okra

NUTRITION: CALORIES: 37, FAT: 0.5 G, CARBS: 7.4 G, PROTEIN: 2 G

10'

10'

4

INGREDIENTS
- 2 cups okra, chopped
- 2 tablespoons fresh dill, chopped
- 1 tablespoon paprika
- 1 cup can tomato, crushed
- Salt and Black pepper to taste

DIRECTIONS
1. Add all ingredients into the inner pot of instant pot and stir well. Seal pot with lid and cook on high for 10 minutes.
2. Once done, allow to release pressure naturally for 5 minutes then release the remaining using quick release. Remove lid.
3. Stir well and serve.

Parsnips with Eggplant

NUTRITION: CALORIES: 98, CARBS: 23 G, PROTEIN: 2.8 G

10'

12'

4

INGREDIENTS
- 2 parsnips, sliced
- 1 cup can tomato, crushed
- ½ teaspoon ground cumin
- 1 tablespoon paprika
- 1 teaspoon garlic, minced
- 1 eggplant, cut into chunks
- ¼ teaspoon dried basil
- Salt and Black pepper to taste

DIRECTIONS
1. Add all ingredients into the instant pot and stir well. Seal pot with lid and cook on high for 12 minutes.
2. Once done, release pressure using quick release. Remove lid. Stir and serve.

Eggplant with Olives

NUTRITION: CALORIES: 105, FAT: 7.4 G, CARBS: 10.4 G, PROTEIN: 1.6 G

INGREDIENTS

- 4 cups eggplants, cut into cubes
- ½ cup vegetable stock
- 1 teaspoon chili powder
- 1 cup olives, pitted and sliced
- 1 onion, chopped
- 1 tablespoon olive oil
- ¼ cup grape tomatoes
- Salt and Black pepper to taste

DIRECTIONS

1. Add oil into the inner pot of instant pot and set the pot on sauté mode.
2. Add onion and sauté for 2 minutes.
3. Add remaining ingredients and stir everything well. Seal pot with lid and cook on high for 12 minutes.
4. Once done, allow to release pressure naturally for 10 minutes then release the remaining using quick release. Remove lid. Stir and serve.

10'
12'
4

Zucchini, Tomato, Potato Ratatouille

NUTRITION: CALORIES: 175, FAT: 1.9 G

INGREDIENTS

- 1 ½ pound of potatoes, cut into cubes
- ½ cup fresh basil
- 28 oz fire-roasted tomatoes, chopped
- 1 onion, chopped
- 4 mushrooms, sliced
- 1 bell pepper, diced
- 12 oz eggplant, diced
- 8 oz zucchini, diced
- 8 oz yellow squash, diced
- Salt and Black pepper to taste

DIRECTIONS

1. Add all ingredients except basil into the instant pot and stir well. Seal pot with lid and cook on high for 10 minutes.
2. Once done, release pressure using quick release. Remove lid.
3. Add basil and stir well and serve.

10'
10'
6

Tomato Stuffed with Cheese and Peppers

NUTRITION: CALORIES: 285, FAT: 10 G, CARBS: 28 G, PROTEIN: 24 G

10'

25'

2

INGREDIENTS
- 4 tomatoes
- ½ pound mixed bell peppers, chopped
- 1 tablespoon olive oil
- 2 garlic cloves, minced
- ½ cup diced onion
- 1 tablespoon chopped oregano
- 1 tablespoon chopped basil
- 1 cup shredded mozzarella cheese
- 1 tablespoon grated Parmesan cheese
- Salt and black pepper to taste

DIRECTIONS
1. Preheat the oven to 370°F. Cut the tops of the tomatoes and scoop out the pulp.
2. Chop the pulp and set it aside.
3. Arrange the tomatoes in a line with a parchment paper baking sheet.
4. Warm the olive oil in a pan over medium heat.
5. Add in garlic, onion, basil, bell peppers, and oregano, and cook for 5 minutes.
6. Sprinkle with salt and pepper. Remove from the heat and mix in tomato pulp and mozzarella cheese. Divide the mixture between the tomatoes and top with Parmesan cheese.
7. Bake for 20 minutes or until the cheese melts. Serve hot.

Loaded Portobello Mushrooms

NUTRITION: CALORIES: 128, FAT: 8 G, CARBS: 5.9 G, PROTEIN: 3 G

10'

45'

4

INGREDIENTS
- 4 portobello mushrooms, stems removed
- 2 cups arugula
- ¼ cup chopped fresh basil leaves
- 2 tablespoons olive oil
- 1 onion, finely chopped
- 1 zucchini, chopped
- ¼ teaspoon dried thyme
- ⅛ teaspoon red pepper flakes
- 2 garlic cloves, minced
- ½ cup grated Parmesan cheese
- Salt and black pepper to taste

DIRECTIONS
1. Preheat the oven to 350°F. Warm olive oil in a skillet over medium heat and sauté onion, arugula, zucchini, thyme, salt, pepper, and red flakes for 5 minutes. Stir in garlic and sauté for 30 seconds. Turn the heat off.
2. Mix in basil and scoop into the mushroom caps and arrange them on a baking sheet.
3. Top with Parmesan cheese and bake for 30-40 minutes, until mushrooms are nice and soft and cheese is melted.

Sumac Chicken with Cauliflower and Carrots

NUTRITION: CALORIES: 401, FAT: 24 G, PROTEIN: 11 G

8'

40'

4

INGREDIENTS
- 3 tablespoons extra-virgin olive oil
- 1 tablespoon ground sumac
- 1 teaspoon kosher salt
- ½ teaspoon ground cumin
- ¼ teaspoon freshly ground black pepper
- 1½ pounds bone-in chicken thighs and drumsticks
- 1 medium cauliflower, cut into 1-inch florets
- 2 carrots
- 1 lemon, cut into ¼-inch-thick slices
- 1 tablespoon lemon juice
- ¼ cup fresh parsley, chopped
- ¼ cup fresh mint, chopped

DIRECTIONS
1. Set the oven to 425°F. Prep a baking sheet using foil.
2. In a large bowl, scourge the olive oil, sumac, salt, cumin, and black pepper.
3. Add the chicken, cauliflower, and carrots and toss until thoroughly coated with the oil and spice mixture.
4. Arrange the cauliflower, carrots, and chicken in a single layer on the baking sheet. Top with the lemon slices. Roast for 40 minutes, tossing the vegetables once halfway through.
5. Sprinkle the lemon juice over the chicken and vegetables and garnish with the parsley and mint.

Harissa Yogurt Chicken Thighs

NUTRITION: CALORIES: 391, FATS: 20 G, PROTEIN: 9 G

9'

23'

4

INGREDIENTS
- ½ cup plain Greek yogurt
- 2 tablespoons harissa
- 1 tablespoon lemon juice
- ¼ teaspoon freshly ground black pepper
- 1½ pounds boneless

DIRECTIONS
1. Mix yogurt, harissa, lemon juice, salt, and black pepper.
2. Add the chicken and mix together. Marinate for at least 15 minutes, and up to 4 hours in the refrigerator.
3. Pull out the chicken thighs from the marinade then arrange them in a single layer on the baking sheet. Roast for 20 minutes, turning the chicken over halfway.
4. Change the oven temperature to broil. Broil the chicken until golden brown in skillets, 2 to 3 minutes.

Braised Chicken with Wild Mushrooms

NUTRITION: CALORIES: 501, FATS: 21 G, PROTEIN: 12 G

11'

28'

4

INGREDIENTS

- ¼ cup dried porcini or morel mushrooms
- ¼ cup olive oil
- 2–3 slices low-salt turkey bacon, chopped
- 1 chicken, cut into pieces
- 1 small celery stalk, diced
- 1 small dried red chili, chopped
- ¼ cup vermouth or white wine
- ¼ cup tomato puree
- ¼ cup low-salt chicken stock
- ½ teaspoon arrowroot
- ¼ cup flat-leaf parsley, chopped
- 4 teaspoons fresh thyme, chopped
- 3 teaspoons fresh tarragon

DIRECTIONS

1. Soak mushrooms in boiling water over them for 20 minutes to soften.
2. Drain and chop, reserving the liquid.
3. Heat the olive oil on medium heat. Stir in bacon and cook until browned and lightly crisp. Drain the bacon on a paper towel.
4. Season the chicken, and add to the oil and bacon drippings.
5. Cook for 10–15 minutes.
6. Add the celery and the chopped chili, and cook for 3–5 minutes.
7. Deglaze the pan with the wine, with a wooden spoon to scrape up the brown bits stuck to the bottom.
8. Add the tomato puree, chicken stock, arrowroot, and mushroom liquid. Close and simmer on low for 45 minutes.
9. Add the fresh chopped herbs and cook for an additional 10 minutes, until the sauce thickens.
10. Season well. Serve with wilted greens or crunchy green beans.

Braised Duck with Fennel Root

NUTRITION: CALORIES: 571, FATS: 24 G, PROTEIN: 15 G

13'

45'

6

INGREDIENTS

- ¼ cup olive oil
- 1 whole duck, cleaned
- 3 teaspoons fresh rosemary
- 2 garlic cloves, minced
- 3 fennel bulbs, cut into chunks
- ½ cup sherry

DIRECTIONS

1. Preheat the oven to 375°F.
2. Cook olive oil in a Dutch oven.
3. Season the duck, including the cavity, with the rosemary, garlic, sea salt, and freshly ground pepper.
4. Place the duck in the oil, and cook it for 10–15 minutes, turning as necessary to brown all sides.
5. Add the fennel bulbs and cook for an additional 5 minutes.
6. Pour the sherry over the duck and fennel, cover and cook in the oven for 30–45 minutes, or until the internal temperature of the duck is 140–150° at its thickest part.
7. Allow the duck to sit for 15 minutes before serving.

Chicken Gyros with Tzatziki

NUTRITION: CALORIES: 289, PROTEIN: 50 G, FAT: 1 G

10'

80'

6

INGREDIENTS

- 1-pound ground chicken breast
- 1 onion
- 2 tablespoons dried rosemary
- 1 tablespoon dried marjoram
- 6 garlic cloves, minced
- ½ teaspoon sea salt
- ¼ teaspoon freshly ground black pepper
- Tzatziki Sauce

DIRECTIONS

1. Preheat the oven to 350°F.
2. In a stand mixer, blend chicken, onion, rosemary, marjoram, garlic, sea salt, and pepper.
3. Press the mixture into a loaf pan. Bake for about 1 hour. Pull out from the oven and set aside for 20 minutes before slicing.
4. Slice the gyro and spoon the tzatziki sauce over the top.

Eggplant Casserole

NUTRITION: CALORIES: 338, PROTEIN: 28 G, FAT: 20 G

10'

45'

8

INGREDIENTS

- 5 tablespoons extra-virgin olive oil
- 1 eggplant
- 1 onion
- 1 green bell pepper
- 1-pound ground turkey
- 3 garlic cloves, minced
- 2 tablespoons tomato paste
- 1 (14-ounce) can chopped tomatoes
- 1 tablespoon Italian seasoning
- 2 teaspoons Worcestershire sauce
- 1 teaspoon dried oregano
- ½ teaspoon ground cinnamon
- 1 cup unsweetened nonfat plain Greek yogurt
- 1 egg, beaten
- ¼ teaspoon freshly ground black pepper
- ¼ teaspoon ground nutmeg
- ¼ cup grated Parmesan cheese
- 2 tablespoons chopped fresh parsley leaves

DIRECTIONS

1. Preheat the oven to 400°F.
2. Preheat skillet over medium-high heat, pour 3 tablespoons
3. Add the eggplant slices and brown for 3 to 4 minutes per side. Transfer to paper towels to drain.
4. Return to the heat and pour the remaining 2 tablespoons of olive oil. Add the onion and green bell pepper. Cook for 5 minutes. Remove from the pan and set aside.
5. Put back to the heat and add the turkey. Cook for about 5 minutes. Cook garlic.
6. Stir in the tomato paste, tomatoes, Italian seasoning, Worcestershire sauce, oregano, and cinnamon. Return the onion and bell pepper to the pan. Cook for 5 minutes, stirring.
7. Scourge yogurt, egg, pepper, nutmeg, and cheese.
8. Using a 9x13-inch baking dish, spread half the meat mixture. Layer with half the eggplant. Add the remaining meat mixture and the remaining eggplant. Spread with the yogurt mixture. Bake for about 20 minutes.
9. Garnish with the parsley and serve.

Dijon and Herb Pork Tenderloin

NUTRITION: CALORIES: 393, PROTEIN: 74 G, FAT: 12 G

10'

30'

6

INGREDIENTS

- ½ cup fresh Italian parsley leaves
- 3 tablespoons fresh rosemary leaves
- 3 tablespoons fresh thyme leaves
- 3 tablespoons Dijon mustard
- 1 tablespoon extra-virgin olive oil
- 4 garlic cloves, minced
- ½ teaspoon sea salt
- ¼ teaspoon freshly ground black pepper
- 1 (1½-pound) pork tenderloin

DIRECTIONS

1. Preheat the oven to 400°F.
2. In a blender, pulse parsley, rosemary, thyme, mustard, olive oil, garlic, sea salt, and pepper. Spread the mixture evenly over the pork and place it on a rimmed baking sheet.
3. Bake for about 20 minutes. Pull out from the oven and put aside for 10 minutes before slicing and serving.

Steak with Red Wine-Mushroom Sauce

NUTRITION: CALORIES: 405, PROTEIN: 33 G, FAT: 22 G

10'

20'

4

INGREDIENTS

For marinade and steak:
- 1 cup dry red wine
- 3 garlic cloves, minced
- 2 tablespoons extra-virgin olive oil
- 1 tablespoon low-sodium soy sauce
- 1 tablespoon dried thyme
- 1 teaspoon Dijon mustard
- 2 tablespoons extra-virgin olive oil
- 1½ pounds skirt steak

For the mushroom sauce:
- 2 tablespoons extra-virgin olive oil
- 1-pound cremini mushrooms
- ½ teaspoon sea salt
- 1 teaspoon dried thyme
- ⅛ teaspoon black pepper
- 2 garlic cloves, minced
- 1 cup dry red wine

DIRECTIONS

For marinade and steak:
1. In a small bowl, whisk the wine, garlic, olive oil, soy sauce, thyme, and mustard. Pour into a resealable bag and add the steak. Refrigerate the steak to marinate for 4 to 8 hours. Remove the steak from the marinade and pat it dry with paper towels.
2. In a big skillet over medium-high heat, warm up olive oil.
3. Cook steak for 4 minutes per side. Pull out the steak from the skillet and put it on a plate tented with aluminum foil to keep warm, while you prepare the mushroom sauce.
4. When the mushroom sauce is ready, slice the steak against the grain into ½-inch-thick slices.

For the mushroom sauce:
5. Preheat the skillet over medium-high heat, and heat the olive oil.
6. Add the mushrooms, sea salt, thyme, and pepper. Cook for about 6 minutes.
7. Cook garlic for 30 seconds.
8. Stir in the wine, and use the side of a wooden spoon to scrape and fold in any browned bits from the bottommost of the skillet. Cook for about 4 minutes. Serve the mushrooms spooned over the steak.

Greek Meatballs

20'

25'

4

INGREDIENTS

- 2 whole-wheat bread slices
- 1¼ pounds ground turkey
- 1 egg
- ¼ cup seasoned whole-wheat bread crumbs
- 3 garlic cloves, minced
- ¼ red onion, grated
- ¼ cup chopped fresh Italian parsley leaves
- 2 tablespoons chopped fresh mint leaves
- 2 tablespoons chopped fresh oregano leaves
- ½ teaspoon sea salt
- ¼ teaspoon freshly ground black pepper

DIRECTIONS

1. Preheat the oven to 350°F.
2. Prep baking sheet with foil.
3. Run the bread under water to wet it, and squeeze out any excess. Rip the wet bread into small pieces and put it in a medium bowl.
4. Add the turkey, egg, bread crumbs, garlic, red onion, parsley, mint, oregano, sea salt, and pepper. Mix well. Form the mixture into ¼-cup-size balls. Place the meatballs on the prepared sheet and bake for about 25 minutes

NUTRITION: CALORIES: 350, PROTEIN: 42 G, FAT: 18 G

Lamb with String Beans

NUTRITION: CALORIES: 439, PROTEIN: 50 G, FAT: 22 G

10'

1h

6

INGREDIENTS

- ¼ cup extra-virgin olive oil
- 6 lamb chops
- 1 teaspoon sea salt
- ½ teaspoon black pepper
- 2 tablespoons tomato paste
- 1 ½ cup hot water
- 1-pound green beans
- 1 onion
- 2 tomatoes

DIRECTIONS

1. In a skillet at medium-high heat, pour 2 tablespoons of olive oil.
2. Season the lamb chops with ½ teaspoon of sea salt and ⅛ teaspoon of pepper. Cook the lamb in the hot oil for about 4 minutes. Transfer the meat to a platter and set it aside.
3. Put back to the heat then put the 2 tablespoons of olive oil. Heat until it shimmers.
4. Blend tomato paste in the hot water. Mix to the hot skillet along with the green beans, onion, tomatoes, and the remaining ½ teaspoon of sea salt and ¼ teaspoon of pepper. Bring to a simmer.
5. Return the lamb chops to the pan. Boil and adjust the heat to medium-low. Simmer for 45 minutes, adding additional water as needed to adjust the thickness of the sauce.

Fish Fillet on Lemons

NUTRITION: CALORIES: 208, FAT: 11 G, PROTEIN: 21 G, CARBS: 2 G

5'

6'

4

INGREDIENTS

- 1 tablespoon extra-virgin olive oil
- Nonstick cooking spray
- ¼ teaspoon freshly ground black pepper
- 4 (4-ounce/ 113-g) fish fillets, such as tilapia, salmon, catfish, cod, or your favorite fish
- 3 to 4 medium lemons
- ¼ teaspoon kosher or sea salt

DIRECTIONS

1. Using paper towels, dry the fillets and let them rest at room temperature for 10 minutes.
2. Meanwhile, coat the cold grill cooking rack with non-stick cooking spray and preheat the grill to 205°C (400°F) or medium-high heat. Or preheat a grill over medium-high heat on the stove.
3. Cut a lemon in half and set half aside.
4. Cut the remaining half of that lemon and the remaining lemons into ¼-inch thick slices. (You should have 12 to 16 lemon slices.)
5. In a small bowl, squeeze 1 tablespoon of juice from the reserved lemon half.
6. Add the oil to the bowl with the lemon juice and mix well.
7. Brush both sides of the fish with the oil mixture and sprinkle evenly with pepper and salt.
8. Carefully arrange the lemon slices on the grill (or grill pan), arranging 3 or 4 slices together in the shape of a fish fillet, and repeat with the remaining slices.
9. Place the fish fillets directly on top of the lemon slices and grill with the lid closed. (If you're grilling on the stove, cover with a large lid or aluminum foil.) Turn the fish halfway through the cooking time only if the fillets are more than half an inch thick. The fish is ready and ready to serve when it begins to separate into flakes (pieces) when gently pressed with a fork.

Tilapia Fillet with Onion and Avocado

NUTRITION: CALORIES: 210, FAT: 10 G, PROTEIN: 25 G, CARBS: 5 G

5'

3'

4

INGREDIENTS

- 1 tablespoon freshly squeezed orange juice
- 4 (4-ounce/113-g) tilapia fillets, more oblong than square, skin-on or skinned
- ¼ cup chopped red onion
- 1 tablespoon extra-virgin olive oil
- ¼ teaspoon kosher or sea salt
- 1 avocado, pitted, skinned, and sliced

DIRECTIONS

1. In a 9-inch glass cake pan, use a fork to mix the oil, orange juice, and salt.
2. Working one fillet at a time, place them in the pan and turn them to cover them from all sides.
3. Arrange the fillets in a wagon wheel formation, so that one end of each fillet is in the center of the plate and the other end is temporarily draped over the edge of the plate.
4. Cover each fillet with 1 tablespoon of onion, then fold the end of the fillet that hangs from the edge above the onion in half. When finished, you should have 4 folded fillets with the crease against the outside edge of the plate and the ends all in the center.
5. Cover the dish with cling film, leaving a small part open at the edge to let the steam escape. Microwave on high for about 3 minutes. The fish is ready when it starts to separate into flakes (pieces) when gently pressed with a fork.
6. Garnish the fillets with the avocado and serve.

Sea Bass Crusted with Moroccan Spices

NUTRITION: CALORIES: 259, FAT: 8 G, PROTEIN: 3 G, CARBS: 49 G

15'

40'

4

INGREDIENTS

- 1 (15-ounce/425-g) can chickpeas, drained and rinsed
- 1 ½ cup low-sodium vegetable broth
- 1½ teaspoons ground turmeric, divided
- ¾ teaspoon saffron
- 1½ pounds (680 g) sea bass fillets, about ½ inch thick
- 8 tablespoons extra-virgin olive oil, divided
- 8 garlic cloves, divided (4 minced cloves and 4 sliced)
- 6 medium baby portobello mushrooms, chopped
- ½ teaspoon ground cumin
- ¼ teaspoon kosher salt
- ¼ teaspoon freshly ground black pepper
- 1 large carrot, sliced on an angle
- 2 sundried tomatoes, thinly sliced (optional)
- 2 tablespoons tomato paste
- ¼ cup white wine
- ½ lemon, juiced
- ½ lemon, cut into thin rounds
- 4 to 5 rosemary sprigs or 2 tablespoons dried rosemary
- 1 tablespoon ground coriander (optional)
- 1 cup sliced artichoke hearts marinated in olive oil
- ½ cup pitted Kalamata olives
- Fresh cilantro for garnish

DIRECTIONS

1. In a small bowl, combine 1 teaspoon of turmeric, saffron and cumin. Season with salt and pepper. Season both sides of the fish with the spice mixture.
2. Add 3 tablespoons of olive oil and work the fish to make sure it is well coated with the spices and olive oil.
3. In a large skillet or skillet, heat 2 tablespoons of olive oil over medium heat until it glistens but smokes. Brown the top of the sea bass for about 1 minute or until golden brown. Remove and set aside.
4. In the same pan, add the minced garlic and cook very briefly, stirring regularly, until it becomes fragrant.
5. Add the mushrooms, carrot, dried tomatoes (if used) and tomato paste. Cook for 3 to 4 minutes over medium heat, stirring often until it becomes fragrant.
6. Add the chickpeas, stock, wine, coriander (if used) and sliced garlic. Stir in the remaining ½ teaspoon of ground turmeric. Turn up the heat if necessary and bring to a boil, then lower the heat to simmer. Cover part of the path and let the sauce simmer for about 20 minutes, until it thickens.
7. Carefully add the seared fish to the pan. Pour some sauce over the fish.
8. Add the artichokes, olives, lemon juice and slices and the sprigs of rosemary. Cook another 10 minutes or until the fish is completely cooked and crumbly. Garnish with fresh cilantro

Classic Escabeche

NUTRITION: CALORIES: 578, FAT: 50 G, PROTEIN: 26 G, CARBS: 13 G

10'

20'

4

INGREDIENTS

- 8 tablespoons extra-virgin olive oil, divided
- 1 bunch asparagus, trimmed and cut into 2-inch pieces
- 1 (13¾-ounce/390-g) can artichoke hearts, drained and quartered
- 4 large garlic cloves, peeled and crushed
- 1 pound (454 g) wild-caught Spanish mackerel fillets, cut into four pieces
- 1 teaspoon salt
- ½ teaspoon freshly ground black pepper
- 2 bay leaves
- ¼ cup red wine vinegar
- ½ teaspoon smoked paprika

DIRECTIONS

1. Sprinkle the fillets with salt and pepper and leave to rest at room temperature for 5 minutes.
2. In a large skillet, heat 2 tablespoons of olive oil over medium-high heat. Add the fish, skin side up, and cook for 5 minutes. Flip and cook 5 minutes on the other side, until golden brown and cooked. Transfer to a serving dish, pour the cooking oil over the fish and cover to keep warm.
3. Heat the remaining 6 tablespoons of olive oil in the same pan over medium heat. Add the asparagus, artichokes, garlic and bay leaves and sauté until the vegetables are tender, 6 to 8 minutes.
4. Using a skimmer, season the fish with the cooked vegetables, keeping the oil in the pan. Add the vinegar and paprika to the oil and blend to mix well. Pour the vinaigrette over the fish and vegetables and let it sit at room temperature for at least 15 minutes, or marinate in the refrigerator for up to 24 hours for a deeper flavor. Remove the bay leaf before serving.

Thyme Whole Roasted Red Snapper

NUTRITION: CALORIES: 345, FAT: 13 G, PROTEIN: 54 G, CARBS: 12 G

5'

45'

4

INGREDIENTS
- 4 or 5 sprigs of thyme
- 3 garlic cloves, sliced
- 1 (2 to 2½ pounds/907 g to 1.1 kg) whole red snapper, cleaned and scaled
- 2 lemons, sliced (about 10 slices)
- 3 tablespoons cold salted butter, cut into small cubes, divided (optional)

DIRECTIONS
1. Preheat the oven to 350°F (180°C).
2. Cut a piece of aluminum foil the size of your pan; put the foil on the baking sheet.
3. Make a horizontal slice across the belly of the fish to create a pocket.
4. Place 3 lemon slices on the aluminum foil and the fish on top of the lemons.
5. Stuff the fish with garlic, thyme, 3 lemon slices and butter. Reserve 3 pieces of butter.
6. Place the reserved 3 pieces of butter on top of the fish and 3 or 4 lemon slices on top of the butter. Gather the foil and seal it to make a pocket around the fish.
7. Place the fish in the oven and cook for 45 minutes. Serve with the remaining fresh lemon slices.

Crispy Fried Sardines

NUTRITION: CALORIES: 794, FAT: 47 G, PROTEIN: 48 G, CARBS: 44 G

5'

5'

4

INGREDIENTS
- 1 teaspoon freshly ground black pepper
- 2 cups flour
- Avocado oil, as needed
- 1½ pounds (680 g) whole fresh sardines, scales removed
- 1 teaspoon salt

DIRECTIONS
1. Preheat a deep skillet over medium heat. Pour in enough oil so that there is about 1 inch in the pan.
2. Season the fish with salt and pepper.
3. Dip the fish in the flour so that it is completely covered.
4. Slowly dip 1 fish at a time, being careful not to overcrowd the pan.
5. Cook for about 3 minutes on each side or until the fish begins to brown on all sides. Serve hot.

103

Fish and Orzo

NUTRITION: CALORIES: 402, FAT: 21 G, CARBS: 21 G, PROTEIN: 31 G

10'

35'

4

INGREDIENTS

- 1 teaspoon garlic, minced
- 1 teaspoon red pepper, crushed
- 2 shallots, chopped
- 1 tablespoon olive oil
- 2 teaspoon anchovy paste
- 2 tablespoon oreganos, chopped
- 2 tablespoons black olives, pitted and chopped
- 2 tablespoons capers, drained
- 15 oz canned tomatoes, crushed
- A pinch of salt and black pepper
- 4 cod fillets, boneless
- 1 oz feta cheese, crumbled
- 1 tablespoons parsley, chopped
- 3 cups chicken stock
- 1 cup orzo pasta
- Zest of 1 lemon, grated

DIRECTIONS

1. Heat a pan with the oil over medium heat, add the garlic, chili and shallot and sauté for 5 minutes.
2. Add the anchovy paste, oregano, black olives, capers, tomatoes, salt and pepper, mix and cook for another 5 minutes.
3. Add the cod fillets, sprinkle with cheese and parsley, place in the oven and cook at 375°F for an extra 15 minutes.
4. Meanwhile, put the broth in a saucepan, bring to a boil over medium heat, add the barley and lemon zest, bring to the boil, cook for 10 minutes, shell with a fork and divide into plates.
5. Top each portion with the fish mix and serve.

104

Spiced Soup with Lentils and Legumes

NUTRITION: CALORIES: 123, FATS: 3 G, CARBS: 19 G, PROTEIN: 5 G

15'

35'

2

INGREDIENTS

- 2 tablespoons extra-virgin olive oil
- 2 garlic cloves, minced
- 4 pcs large celery stalks, diced
- 2 pcs large onions, diced
- 6 cups water
- 1 teaspoon cumin
- ¾ teaspoon turmeric
- ½ teaspoon cinnamon
- ½ teaspoon fresh ginger, grated
- 1 cup dried lentils, rinsed and sorted
- 1 (16 oz) can chickpeas (garbanzo beans), drained and rinsed
- 3 pcs ripe tomatoes, cubed
- ½ lemon, juice
- ½ cup fresh cilantro or parsley, chopped
- Salt to taste

DIRECTIONS

1. Heat the olive oil and sauté the garlic, celery, and onion for 5 minutes in a large stockpot placed over medium heat.
2. Pour in the water. Add the spices and lentils. Cover the stockpot and simmer for 40 minutes until the lentils are tender.
3. Add the chickpeas and tomatoes. (Pour more water and additional spices, if desired.) Simmer for 15 minutes over low heat.
4. Pour in the lemon juice and stir the soup. Add the cilantro or parsley and salt to taste.

Brown Rice Pilaf with Golden Raisins

NUTRITION: CALORIES: 320, FAT: 7 G, CARBS: 61 G, PROTEIN: 6 G

5'

15'

6

INGREDIENTS

- 1 tablespoon extra-virgin olive oil
- 1 cup chopped onion (about ½ medium onion)
- ½ cup shredded carrot (about 1 medium carrot)
- 1 teaspoon ground cumin
- ½ teaspoon ground cinnamon
- 2 cups instant brown rice
- 1 ¾ cup 100% orange juice
- ¼ cup water
- 1 cup golden raisins
- ½ cup shelled pistachios

DIRECTIONS

1. In a medium saucepan over medium-high heat, heat the oil. Add the onion and cook for 5 minutes, stirring frequently.
2. Add the carrot, cumin, and cinnamon, and cook for 1 minute, stirring frequently. Stir in the rice, orange juice, and water.
3. Bring to a boil, cover, then lower the heat to medium-low. Simmer for 7 minutes, or until the rice is cooked through and the liquid is absorbed. Stir in the raisins, pistachios, and chives (if using) and serve.

CHAPTER 7

Snack recipes

Mediterranean Pasta

NUTRITION: CALORIES: 366, PROTEIN: 27 G, CARBS: 42 G, FAT: 65 G

5'

15'

3

INGREDIENTS

- 1 tablespoon kosher salt plus 1 teaspoon, divided
- 6 oz whole wheat angel hair pasta whole wheat spaghetti, or similar whole wheat noodles (I recommend DeLallo whole wheat pasta)
- 4 garlic cloves
- 2 cups grape tomatoes or cherry tomatoes
- 1 can quartered artichoke hearts (14 oz)
- 1 can whole pitted black olives (6 oz)
- 3 tablespoons good-quality olive oil
- ½ teaspoon ground black pepper
- ¼-½ teaspoon crushed red pepper flakes
- ¼ cup freshly squeezed lemon juice about 1 lemon
- ¼ cup freshly grated Parmesan cheese
- ¼ cup fresh Italian parsley chopped

DIRECTIONS

1. Bring 1 tablespoon salt to a boil in a big saucepan of water. Cook the pasta until it is al dente (firm to the bite). Drain all except 12 cups of pasta water.
2. Prep your veggies and additional ingredients while the water boils and the pasta cooks: mince the garlic; halve the cherry tomatoes; drain and roughly cut the artichokes; drain and slice the olives in half. The dish moves rapidly as the veggies begin to cook, so be prepared.
3. In a large pan, heat the olive oil over medium-high heat. Combine the tomatoes, garlic, 1 teaspoon salt, pepper, and crushed red pepper flakes in a mixing bowl. Cook, stirring regularly, for 1 to 2 minutes, or until the garlic is aromatic and the tomatoes have broken down and released some juices into the oil.
4. Toss the spaghetti in the skillet to coat it. Combine the artichokes and olives in a bowl. Pour the lemon juice over the spaghetti and toss to combine.
5. Toss for another 1 to 2 minutes, or until warmed through. If the pasta appears to be too dry, a dash of the leftover pasta water can be added to soften it up. Taste and season with salt and pepper to taste. Remove from the heat and top with Parmesan cheese and parsley. Once more, toss and enjoy

Nonna's Spaghetti and Broccoli

NUTRITION: CALORIES: 543, PROTEIN: 37 G, CARBS: 52 G, FAT: 55 G

10'

1h 30'

2

INGREDIENTS

- 3 tablespoons salt
- 1 pound spaghetti broken into 2-3" pieces
- ½ cup olive oil
- 2 (12 oz) packages fresh broccoli florets
- 8-10 garlic cloves peeled, crushed, and minced
- ¼ teaspoon freshly grated black pepper
- 1 ½-2 cups grated Romano cheese or more to taste
- 2 cups shredded mozzarella or more to taste
- ½ cup shredded Parmesan
- ¼ teaspoon crushed red pepper flakes optional

DIRECTIONS

1. Fill an 8-quart saucepan to slightly below ¾ capacity with water. Bring to a rolling boil, stirring in the salt.
2. Combine the pasta, oil, garlic, pepper, and broccoli in a mixing bowl.
3. Return the mixture to a boil and cook for another 2-3 minutes. Cover the saucepan, turn off the heat, and let the mixture sit for about an hour and a half, stirring every 15 minutes until the pasta is cooked through and most of the liquid has been absorbed.
4. Stir in the Romano cheese for 45 minutes, until it has melted and is uniformly distributed. As soon as the pasta is done, add the remaining cheeses and toss until melted before servings.
5. If preferred, top with more grated Parmesan and serve with a slice of warm crusty bread.

One-Pot Creamy Hummus Pasta

NUTRITION: CALORIES: 653, PROTEIN: 43 G, CARBS: 67 G, FAT: 30 G

5'

15'

3

INGREDIENTS

- 8 oz dry linguine
- ¼ cup sun-dried tomatoes packed in oil drained
- 1 tablespoon sun-dried tomato oil
- 3 garlic cloves diced
- ¾ cup hummus + more for leftovers
- 1 cup pasta water
- 2 cups baby spinach
- Salt and pepper to taste
- Red pepper flakes optional

DIRECTIONS

1. A large pot of water should be brought to a boil. Cook for 10-12 minutes, or until pasta is tender. Drain the pasta, keeping 1 cup of the cooking liquid.
2. Return the empty saucepan to the burner and heat it over medium heat. Toss in the sun-dried tomatoes, oil, and garlic in a pan. 2 minutes of sautéing Stir together the hummus and pasta in the pan.
3. Slowly drizzle in ¼ cup of pasta water at a time until the sauce achieves the desired consistency. Add the spinach and cook until it has wilted (approx. 1 minute). Season to taste with salt and pepper.
4. Serve right away and enjoy!

Ingredient Chicken Feta Pasta

NUTRITION: CALORIES: 446, PROTEIN: 76 G, CARBS: 55 G, FAT: 25 G

5'

30'

4

INGREDIENTS

- 2 tablespoons extra-virgin olive oil
- 1 ½ pound boneless skinless breasts, split in half
- 1 teaspoon kosher salt divided
- ¼ teaspoon freshly ground black pepper
- 2 cans diced tomatoes with basil, garlic, and oregano (14.5-ounce cans)
- 2 cups water
- 1-pound whole wheat fettuccini pasta or substitute another long, straight pasta such as spaghetti
- 4 oz reduced-fat feta cheese divided
- Finely chopped fresh basil optional

DIRECTIONS

1. Heat the olive oil in a large saucepan or Dutch oven with a cover over high heat for 1 minute, then add the chicken breast halves. 12 teaspoon salt and black pepper, to taste.
2. Cook the chicken for 8 minutes on one side, moving it around a bit in the pan to keep it from sticking but not too much so that a good crust forms. If the chicken appears to be cooking too rapidly, reduce the heat as required.
3. Cook for another 5 minutes, until the chicken is cooked through, then flip and season with the remaining 12 teaspoon salt.
4. Toss in the chopped tomatoes and a splash of water. Cook, uncovered, for 5 minutes after adding the pasta. Cover and cook for another 10 minutes.
5. Remove the cover and whisk in three-quarters of the feta cheese. Stir one more, then cook for another 5 minutes uncovered. Serve hot, with the leftover feta cheese and fresh basil on top.

One-Pot Creamy Tuscan Garlic Spaghetti

NUTRITION: CALORIES: 754, PROTEIN: 49 G, CARBS: 75 G FAT: 15 G

INGREDIENTS

- 12 oz spaghetti noodles
- 1 cup sliced mushrooms
- 2 whole roasted red peppers - (or contents of one jar), chopped
- 1 medium onion - chopped
- 2 cups baby spinach leaves
- 1 tablespoon minced garlic
- 1 tablespoon Italian seasoning
- 1 teaspoon salt - or to taste
- 4 cups water
- ¼ cup olive oil
- ½ cup heavy cream
- ⅔ cup shaved or shredded parmesan cheese
- Freshly cracked black pepper to taste

DIRECTIONS

1. In a large saucepan, mix together the spaghetti, mushrooms, red peppers, onion, spinach, garlic, Italian seasoning, salt, water, and olive oil. Over medium-high heat, bring to a boil.
2. Allow for 10-12 minutes of cooking time, or until almost all of the water has been absorbed and the noodles are fully cooked and soft.
3. Over medium heat, whisk in the heavy cream and parmesan cheese until the sauce thickens and the noodles are covered for about 3-5 minutes.
4. Serve with more parmesan cheese, crushed black pepper, and fresh herbs (such as thyme or parsley) if preferred.

10-Minute Mediterranean Vegan Pasta

NUTRITION: CALORIES: 876, PROTEIN: 43 G, CARBS: 51 G, FAT: 32 G

INGREDIENTS

- 10 oz of your favorite pasta (I used gluten-free)
- 1 cup hummus
- ⅓ cup water
- 5 garlic cloves, minced or pressed
- ½ cup olives
- ½ cup walnuts
- 2 tablespoons dried cranberries, optional
- Salt and pepper to taste

DIRECTIONS

1. Cook the pasta according to the package instructions.
2. Prepare the hummus sauce while the pasta is cooking: mix the hummus, water, and garlic, then season with salt and pepper. Finally, add the olives, walnuts, and dried cranberries, if desired. Drain the pasta and toss it with the sauce once it's done.

Best Vegan Chili with Quinoa

NUTRITION: CALORIES: 442, PROTEIN: 54 G, CARBS: 66 G, FAT: 21 G

15'

30'

4

INGREDIENTS

- ½ cup quinoa uncooked
- 1 cup water
- 2 tablespoons Greek extra virgin olive oil I used Early Harvest EVOO
- ½ large yellow onion chopped
- 5 garlic cloves minced
- 2 carrots peeled and chopped
- ½ large green bell pepper chopped
- 1 (16 oz/453.59 g) can chop tomatoes with juice
- 4 cups low-sodium vegetable broth
- 2 ½ teaspoon chili powder
- 1 teaspoon sweet paprika
- 1 teaspoon ground cumin
- ½ teaspoon ground allspice
- Salt and pepper
- 1 (15 oz/425.24 g) can black beans drained and rinsed
- 1 (15 oz/425.24 g) can kidney beans drained and rinsed
- ½ cup/25 g chopped fresh cilantro
- ¼ cup/5 g chopped fresh parsley
- 1 large lime juice of
- 1 jalapeño sliced (optional)

DIRECTIONS

1. Combine quinoa and water in a small saucepan. Cook for 10 to 15 minutes over medium heat, or until the water is absorbed (quinoa will be partly cooked). Remove from heat and put aside.
2. 2 tablespoons extra-virgin olive oil, heated in a large skillet or pot over medium heat until shimmering but not smoking. Combine the onions, garlic, carrots, and bell peppers in a large mixing bowl. Cook, turning occasionally, for 4 minutes or until softened.
3. Toss in the tomatoes, stock, and seasonings. Salt and pepper to taste. Bring the water to a boil.
4. Add the black beans, kidney beans, and quinoa that haven't been fully cooked. Reduce to low heat and cook for 25 minutes.
5. Remove the pan from the heat. Combine cilantro, parsley, and lemon juice in a mixing bowl. Add a liberal drizzle of Early Harvest extra virgin olive oil and jalapeño slices, if used, to servings dishes. Enjoy!

Shrimp Pasta with Lemon Garlic Sauce

NUTRITION: CALORIES: 656, PROTEIN: 56 G, CARBS: 53 G, FAT: 21 G

10'

20'

4

INGREDIENTS

- 1-pound jumbo shrimp, peeled and deveined, 16/20 count
- ½ teaspoon kosher salt, plus more as needed
- ¼ teaspoon black pepper, freshly grated, plus more if needed
- 3 tablespoons olive oil, divided
- 2 cups zucchini, ⅛-inch-thick slices
- 1 cup grape tomatoes, cut in half
- 2 garlic cloves, minced
- ⅛ teaspoon red pepper flakes
- Zest of one lemon, about 1 teaspoon
- 2 tablespoons lemon juice
- 8 oz pappardelle pasta, fresh or dried
- 1 tablespoon Italian parsley, chopped

DIRECTIONS

1. For the pasta, bring 3 to 4 quarts of salted water to a boil. Prepare the shrimp while the water is coming to a boil.
2. Stir in ¼ teaspoon salt and ¼ teaspoon peppers to season shrimp.
3. 1 tablespoon oil, heated in a large sauté pan over medium heat
4. Sauté the zucchini slices for 4 minutes, or until they are barely soft.
5. Sauté the sliced grape tomatoes for 2 minutes, or until they start to soften.
6. Toss the veggies with ¼ teaspoon of salt and whisk to mix. Place in a medium-sized bowl and set aside.
7. Turn the heat to medium-low and add 2 tablespoons of oil to the pan.
8. Stir in the garlic and red pepper flakes, and simmer for 2 minutes to avoid browning or burning the garlic. Turn the heat to low if necessary to allow the garlic to cook gently for the flavors to soak into the oil.
9. Add the seasoned shrimp while keeping the heat on medium-low. Cook for 2 to 3 minutes on each side, or until the color is barely pink.
10. Toss in the lemon juice and zest and whisk to mix.
11. Return the cooked zucchini and tomatoes to the pan with the shrimp and stir to mix.
12. Add the pasta to the boiling water and cook until cooked, according to the package recommendations.
13. Drain the pasta and combine it with the shrimp and veggies in a large mixing bowl. As needed, season with extra salt and pepper. Parsley is chopped and sprinkled on top.

114

One-Pot Spinach and Feta Macaroni and Cheese

NUTRITION: CALORIES: 964, PROTEIN: 67 G, CARBS: 55 G FAT: 35 G

5'

20'

4

INGREDIENTS

- 2 tablespoons olive oil
- 1 yellow onion, diced
- A pinch of salt
- 2 garlic cloves, minced
- 2 fresh tomatoes, diced
- 1 bag (8 to 10 oz) fresh baby spinach
- ½ cup crumbled feta cheese
- ½ cup cubed white cheddar cheese
- ¼ cup part-skim shredded mozzarella cheese
- 2 cups elbow macaroni (whenever possible, use whole grain/multigrain macaroni)
- 1 cup low-sodium vegetable broth
- 1 cup unsweetened almond milk
- ½ teaspoon Italian seasoning
- Salt and fresh ground pepper, to taste
- Parsley for garnish

DIRECTIONS

1. In a large pan, heat the olive oil over medium-high heat. (If using a lidded pan, add the onions and a bit of salt and simmer for 2 to 3 minutes, or until softened.)
2. Cook for another 30 seconds, or until the garlic is aromatic.
3. Combine the tomatoes, spinach, cheeses, macaroni, vegetable broth, milk, and spices in a large mixing bowl.
4. Stir to incorporate and bring to a boil, constantly stirring.
5. Reduce heat to medium-low, cover, and simmer for another 12 to 15 minutes, or until pasta is done. To avoid sticking, stir often, roughly every 3 minutes.
6. Remove the pan from the heat and give it a good swirl.
7. Serve immediately with a parsley garnish.

115

One-Pot Buffalo Chicken Pasta

NUTRITION: CALORIES: 721, PROTEIN: 53 G, CARBS: 75 G, FAT: 43 G

10'

20'

4

INGREDIENTS

- 8 oz pasta (such as penne or rigatoni)
- 3 cups cooked chicken, cut into strips
- 2 cups chicken broth
- 1 cup diced green onions
- 1 cup thinly sliced celery
- ½ cup buffalo sauce
- ½ cup blue cheese crumbles plus extra for garnish

DIRECTIONS

1. Combine all of the ingredients in a saucepan. Bring to a boil over medium heat, stirring constantly. Reduce the heat to low and cook for 15 minutes, or until the pasta is tender but still firm. Stir once more.
2. Serve with more blue cheese crumbles on top.

Drunken Wild Mushroom Pasta

NUTRITION: CALORIES: 352, PROTEIN: 57 G, CARBS: 32 G, FAT: 10 G

5'

30'

6-8

INGREDIENTS

- 3 tablespoons olive oil
- 26 oz assortment of wild mushrooms, sliced (cremini, shitake, oyster, baby bella, whatever you want)
- 1 red onion, diced
- 4 garlic cloves, minced
- 1 teaspoon sea salt
- 2 tablespoons sherry cooking wine
- 2 ½ teaspoons fresh thyme, diced
- 1 pound Dream fields linguine pasta
- 6 oz goat cheese
- ¾ cup reserved pasta cooking liquid
- Salt to taste
- ¼ cup hazelnuts, chopped

DIRECTIONS

1. A big pot of water should be brought to a boil.
2. Preheat the oven to 350°F and a large pan to medium-high heat.
3. Toss in the mushrooms and olive oil. Cook for 7-10 minutes, or until the mushrooms begin to brown.
4. Season with salt and pepper after adding the onions and garlic. For 3-4 minutes, sauté and stir onions.
5. Cook until the liquid has evaporated, then add the sherry cooking wine. Finish on a new timer and set it away.
6. Toss the noodles into the boiling water. Cook until the pasta is al dente (according to package instructions)
7. Drain the rest of the pasta boiling liquid and set aside ¾ cup.
8. In a large mixing bowl, combine the noodles, wild mushroom combination, goat cheese, and cooking liquid. Toss to combine all of the ingredients until the goat cheese is thoroughly melted.
9. Hazelnuts, chopped, on top!

117

Shrimp Spaghetti Aglio Olio

NUTRITION: CALORIES: 298, PROTEIN: 45 G, CARBS: 44 G, FAT: 22 G

5'

20'

INGREDIENTS
- 250 g spaghetti
- 3 tablespoons olive oil
- 1 tablespoon garlic finely minced
- 1 teaspoon chili flakes
- 250 g large shrimp or prawns cleaned and de-veined
- 1 tablespoon parsley chopped
- Parmesan grated for topping
- Salt to taste

DIRECTIONS
1. Cook pasta in salted water until al dente, as directed on the box. ¼ cup of pasta water should be set aside.
2. In a pan, heat the olive oil and add the garlic. At a low temperature, sauté the garlic until it's aromatic. Add the prawns and the chili flakes. After 3–4 minutes of cooking time for the shrimp, bring the pasta water to a boil in the pan.
3. Add the drained pasta and stir in the sauce after the pasta water has decreased a little and thickened into a sauce (approximately 2 minutes). Combine the parsley and parmesan cheeses in a mixing bowl. Serve right away.

4

118

15-Minute Caprese Pasta Recipe

NUTRITION: CALORIES: 433, PROTEIN: 47 G, CARBS: 55 G, FAT: 15 G

5'

10'

INGREDIENTS
- 1-pound Angel Hair pasta
- 4 tablespoons olive oil
- 1 small onion, finely chopped
- 4 garlic cloves, finely minced
- 3 cups cherry tomatoes, quartered
- 2 handfuls fresh basil, large, thinly sliced
- 8 oz mozzarella cheese, sliced into small cubes
- 1 tablespoon balsamic vinegar, optional
- Salt and freshly ground black pepper, to taste
- Crushed red pepper flakes, optional
- Grated parmesan cheese to serve

DIRECTIONS
1. Bring a big saucepan of water to a boil with a liberal amount of salt. Follow the package directions for cooking the pasta. Drain, reserving ½ cup of the cooking liquid.
2. While the pasta is cooking, prepare the following: In a large skillet, heat 1 tablespoon olive oil over medium heat. Sauté the onion and garlic for 3 minutes, or until softened.
3. Toss the remaining ingredients with the pasta:
4. Toss the spaghetti with the sauce in the heated pan until it is uniformly covered.
5. Toss in the tomatoes with the remaining 3 tablespoons of olive oil for another minute.
6. Add a couple of tablespoons of pasta boiling water, just enough to keep it moist.
7. Season to taste with the basil, mozzarella, and balsamic vinegar (if using).
8. Serve immediately with grated parmesan cheese.

4

Mediterranean One-Pot Pasta

NUTRITION: CALORIES: 489, PROTEIN: 65 G, CARBS: 42 G, FAT: 35 G

10'

15'

4

INGREDIENTS

- ⅛-ounce gluten-free pasta corn/quinoa or chickpea/lentil*
- 3 cups water boiling
- 1 can vegetable broth
- 1 can fire-roasted tomatoes
- 1 can artichoke hearts drained
- 1 cup black olives
- ½ purple onion sliced
- 2 tablespoons fresh thyme sub 1 teaspoon dried thyme
- 1 teaspoon cumin
- Sea salt and black pepper to taste
- Parmesan to serve, optional
- Basil to serve, optional

DIRECTIONS

1. In a big saucepan, bring 3 cups of water to a boil. Combine the pasta, vegetable broth, onions, tomatoes, artichoke hearts, olives, thyme, and cumin in a large mixing bowl.
2. Allow the pasta to return to a boil over high heat, stirring constantly while it cooks.
3. Maintain a boil for the pasta, but decrease the heat slightly while it cooks. To keep the pasta from sticking together or clinging to the bottom of the pot, toss it occasionally with tongs.
4. Keep an eye on the pasta as the water reduces and turns into a sauce. If the pasta needs extra time to cook, dilute the sauce by adding ½ cup of boiling water at a time.
5. Season with salt and pepper after the sauce has reduced.
6. To avoid the pasta from overcooking in the broth, take it from the saucepan and quickly transfer it to plates.
7. Serve immediately, garnished with fresh herbs or parmesan cheese.

120

Farfalle with Tuna, Lemon, and Fennel

NUTRITION: CALORIES: 442, PROTEIN: 54 G, CARBS: 66 G, FAT: 21 G

10'

20'

4

INGREDIENTS

- 6 oz dried whole grain farfalle (bow-tie) pasta
- 1 (5 oz) can solid white tuna (packed in oil)
- 1 Olive oil
- 1 cup fennel, thinly sliced (1 medium bulb)
- 2 garlic cloves, minced
- ½ teaspoon crushed red pepper
- ¼ teaspoon salt
- 2 (14.5 oz) cans no-salt-added diced tomatoes, undrained
- 2 tablespoons snipped fresh Italian (flat leaf) parsley
- 1 teaspoon lemon peel, finely shredded

DIRECTIONS

1. Drain pasta and cook according to package directions, avoiding salt. Return the spaghetti to the pan and cover to keep it heated. Meanwhile, drain the tuna and set aside the oil. Add additional olive oil to make 3 tablespoons total if required. Set aside flakes of tuna.
2. 3 tablespoons saved oil, heated over medium heat in a medium saucepan Cook, stirring periodically, for 3 minutes with fennel. Cook and stir for 1 minute, or until garlic is golden.
3. Tomatoes are added last. Bring to a boil, then turn off the burner. Cover and cook for 5 to 6 minutes, or until the mixture thickens. Stir in the tuna and cook for another minute or so, uncovered, until the tuna is well cooked.
4. Pour the tuna mixture over the spaghetti and toss to incorporate. Parsley and lemon peel should be sprinkled on top of each dish.

121

Easy Italian Shrimp Tortellini Bake

NUTRITION: CALORIES: 573, PROTEIN: 55 G, CARBS: 65 G, FAT: 40 G

15'

5'

6

INGREDIENTS

- ¾ pound jumbo shrimp, peeled and deveined
- 2 (9 oz) packages of whole wheat cheese tortellini (use regular if you're not a fan of whole wheat)
- 2 - 2 ½ cup marinara or spaghetti sauce
- ½ - ¾ cup shredded mozzarella cheese
- 1 ½ tablespoon parmesan cheese
- 2 tablespoons extra virgin olive oil
- Salt and pepper to taste
- Fresh chopped parsley for garnish

DIRECTIONS

1. Preheat the broiler to high.
2. Set aside the tortellini after cooking it according to the package recommendations. Toss the shrimp with olive oil after seasoning with salt and pepper. Cook for 3-5 minutes each side in an oven-safe pan over medium heat, or until pink. Remove the pan from the heat and set it aside. You may now turn off the stove because you've finished using it.
3. Place the cooked tortellini in the skillet after tossing them with the marinara sauce. Sprinkle the parmesan cheese, then the mozzarella cheese, on top of the shrimp.
4. Broil until the cheese is slightly browned and bubbling.

Pasta Fagioli

NUTRITION: CALORIES: 241, PROTEIN: 37 G, CARBS: 33 G, FAT: 21 G

10'

35'

6

INGREDIENTS

- 2 tablespoons olive oil
- 1 small yellow onion chopped
- 1 medium carrot chopped
- 1 celery stalk chopped
- 3 garlic cloves minced
- 2 bay leaves
- 3 (15 oz) cans diced tomatoes
- 2 (14.5 oz) cans vegetable broth
- 2 (14 oz) cans cannellini beans, rinsed and drained
- 1 small parmesan rind
- 1 teaspoon dried thyme
- 1 teaspoon dried basil
- ½ teaspoon dried rosemary
- Dash of crushed red pepper
- 1 cup dried ditalini or other small pasta
- ¼ cup chopped flat-leaf parsley
- Grated Parmesan cheese for servings, optional

DIRECTIONS

1. Heat the olive oil in a big saucepan over medium-high heat. Add the onion, carrot, and celery and cook for 5 minutes, or until softened. Cook for another 2 minutes after adding the garlic. Add the bay leaves and mix well.
2. Combine the tomatoes, vegetable broth, beans, and parmesan rind in a large mixing bowl. Combine the thyme, basil, rosemary, and crushed red pepper in a mixing bowl. Salt and black pepper to taste. Allow for a 15-minute simmer on low heat.
3. Increase the heat to medium and stir in the pasta. Cook for 8-10 minutes, or until pasta is cooked. Add the parsley and mix well. Remove the bay leaves and peel them from the parmesan cheese.
4. Serve in dishes with grated Parmesan cheese on top, if preferred.

Sweet Potato Noodles with Almond Sauce

NUTRITION: CALORIES: 555, PROTEIN: 58 G, CARBS: 54 G, FAT: 35 G

5'

15'

4

INGREDIENTS

Almond Sauce:
- 2 tablespoons extra-virgin olive oil
- 3 shallots, minced
- 2 garlic cloves, minced
- 3 tablespoons all-purpose flour
- 2 cups plain, unsweetened almond milk
- 2 tablespoons Dijon mustard
- Salt and freshly ground black pepper

Sweet Potato Noodles:
- 2 tablespoons extra-virgin olive oil
- 3 sweet potatoes, cut into noodles (made using a spiralizer)
- 4 cups roughly torn kale
- Salt and freshly ground black pepper
- ½ cup toasted, salted almonds, roughly chopped

DIRECTIONS

Make the almond sauce:
1. Heat the olive oil in a medium saucepan over medium heat. Sauté the shallots and garlic for 1 minute, or until aromatic.
2. Cook, stirring frequently, for 1 minute after adding the flour. Whisk in the almond milk regularly to avoid lumps appearing in the sauce. Stir constantly over medium heat until the mixture reaches a simmer. Cook for 4 to 5 minutes on low heat.
3. Season the sauce with salt and pepper after whisking in the Dijon mustard. While you cook the noodles, cover the sauce and keep it warm over low heat.

Make the sweet potato noodles:
4. Heat the olive oil in a large sauté pan over medium heat. Add the sweet potato noodles and cook, stirring periodically, for 5 to 6 minutes, or until they are nearly soft.
5. Toss in the kale until it wilts. Toss in the sauce until the noodles are thoroughly covered.
6. Add the almonds just before servings and mix to mix. Salt and pepper to taste. Serve right away.

124

Shrimp and Pasta Stew

NUTRITION: CALORIES: 875, PROTEIN: 44 G, CARBS: 56 G, FAT: 25 G

15'

30'

6-8

INGREDIENTS

- 2 tablespoons extra-virgin olive oil
- 2 cups peeled pearl onions (frozen is fine)
- 3 celery stalks, chopped
- 3 garlic cloves, minced
- ½ cup white wine
- 1 tablespoon hot paprika
- A pinch cayenne pepper
- 2 tablespoons lemon zest
- Kosher salt
- Freshly ground black pepper
- One 28-ounce can crush tomatoes
- 4 cups seafood or vegetable broth
- 2 ½ cups pasta (see finishing touches)
- 1 ½ pounds shrimp, peeled and deveined
- 3 cups roughly chopped kale
- Lemon zest, for garnish
- Chopped fresh parsley, for garnish

DIRECTIONS

1. Warm the olive oil in a big saucepan over medium heat. Sauté the onions and celery for 5 to 6 minutes, or until tender. Cook for another minute, or until the garlic is aromatic.
2. Pour in the wine and bring to low heat. Cook for 6 to 7 minutes, or until the liquid has been reduced by half. Paprika, cayenne pepper, lemon zest, salt, and pepper to taste. Simmer for another 1 to 2 minutes, or until aromatic.
3. Return to low heat and add the tomatoes and broth. Stir in the pasta and simmer for 5 minutes, or until it just begins to get tender. Reduce the heat to low, add the shrimp and kale, and continue to cook, stirring occasionally, for 4 to 5 minutes, or until the pasta is soft, the shrimp are cooked through, and the kale has wilted.
4. To serve, spoon the stew into serving dishes and top with lemon zest and parsley. With crusty bread, serve.

125

Cold Lemon Zoodles

NUTRITION: CALORIES: 754, PROTEIN: 57 G, CARBS: 32 G, FAT: 45 G

20'

0'

5

INGREDIENTS

- 1 lemon, zested and juiced
- ½ teaspoon Dijon mustard
- ½ teaspoon garlic powder
- ⅓ cup olive oil
- Salt and freshly ground black pepper
- 3 medium zucchinis, cut into noodles (using a gadget like this)
- 1 bunch radishes, thinly sliced
- 1 tablespoon chopped fresh thyme

DIRECTIONS

1. Combine the lemon zest, lemon juice, mustard, and garlic powder in a small mixing basin.
2. Whisk in the olive oil in a slow, steady stream. Salt and pepper to taste.
3. Toss the zucchini noodles with the radishes in a large mixing basin. Toss in the dressing until the vegetables are well covered.
4. Garnish with fresh thyme and serve right away.

Pasta Alla Norma with Eggplant, Basil and Pecorino

NUTRITION: CALORIES: 675, PROTEIN: 85 G, CARBS: 69 G, FAT: 55 G

20'

40'

4

INGREDIENTS

- 4 tablespoons extra-virgin olive oil
- 1 large eggplant, sliced into 1-inch strips
- Kosher salt and freshly ground black pepper
- 1 sweet onion, thinly sliced
- 3 garlic cloves, peeled and crushed
- 1 28-ounce can crush tomatoes
- 1 teaspoon crushed red pepper flakes
- ¾ teaspoon dried oregano
- 1-pound bite-size dry pasta, like rigatoni or macaroni
- ¼ cup chopped fresh parsley
- ¼ cup chopped fresh basil
- ½ cup grated pecorino or ricotta salata cheese

DIRECTIONS

1. Heat the olive oil in a large sauté pan over medium heat. Cook the eggplant in batches until golden brown on all sides. Place the eggplant on a big platter and remove it from the pan. Season with salt and pepper to taste.
2. Add the onion to the same pan and cook until soft, about 4 minutes. Add the garlic and cook for another minute, or until fragrant.
3. Add the tomatoes and heat to a low boil. Season with salt and pepper after adding the red pepper flakes and oregano. Simmer for 15 to 20 minutes, or until the sauce's taste has developed and concentrated significantly.
4. Bring a big saucepan of salted water to a boil over high heat while the sauce simmers. Add the pasta and cook according to the package directions. Drain thoroughly.
5. Toss in the pasta and eggplant with the sauce. Toss in the parsley, basil, and pecorino or ricotta salata until everything is completely combined.

Tortellini with Pesto and Broccoli

NUTRITION: CALORIES: 876, PROTEIN: 43 G, CARBS: 51 G, FAT: 32 G

INGREDIENTS

- 140 g Tender stem broccoli, cut into short lengths
- 250 g fresh tortellini
- 3 tablespoons pesto (fresh if you can get it)
- 2 tablespoons toasted pine nuts
- 1 tablespoon balsamic vinegar
- 8 cherry tomatoes, halved

DIRECTIONS

1. A big pot of water should be brought to a boil. Simmer for 2 minutes after adding the broccoli, then add the tortellini and cook for another 2 minutes, or according to package directions. Everything should be drained and rinsed under cold water until cool, then poured into a basin.
2. Combine the pesto, pine nuts, and balsamic vinegar in a mixing bowl.
3. Add the tomatoes, put them into containers, and set them aside to cool. To get the maximum flavor from the tomatoes and pesto, bring the salad to room temperature in the morning.

Spinach Pesto Pasta

NUTRITION: CALORIES: 213, FAT: 17.3 G, CARBS: 9.5 G, PROTEIN: 7.4 G

INGREDIENTS

- 8 oz whole-grain pasta
- ⅓ cup mozzarella cheese, grated
- ½ cup pesto
- 5 oz fresh spinach
- 1 ¾ cup water
- 8 oz mushrooms, chopped
- 1 tablespoon olive oil
- Pepper
- Salt

DIRECTIONS

1. Add oil into the inner pot of instant pot and set the pot on sauté mode.
2. Add mushrooms and sauté for 5 minutes.
3. Add water and pasta and stir well.
4. Seal pot with lid and cook on high for 5 minutes.
5. Once done, release pressure using quick release. Remove lid.
6. Stir in remaining ingredients and serve.

Authentic Pasta e Fagioli

NUTRITION: CALORIES: 486; FAT: 8.3 G; CARBS: 95 G; PROTEIN: 12.4 G

6'

15'

4

INGREDIENTS
- 2 tablespoons olive oil
- 1 teaspoon garlic, pressed
- 4 small-sized potatoes, peeled and diced
- 1 parsnip, chopped
- 1 carrot, chopped
- 1 celery rib, chopped
- 1 leek, chopped
- 1 (6 oz) can tomato paste
- 4 cups water
- 2 vegetable bouillon cubes
- 8 oz cannellini beans, soaked overnight
- 6 oz elbow pasta
- ½ teaspoon oregano
- ½ teaspoon basil
- ½ teaspoon fennel seeds
- Sea salt to taste
- ¼ teaspoon freshly cracked black pepper
- 2 tablespoons Italian parsley, roughly chopped

DIRECTIONS
1. Press the "Sauté" button to preheat your Instant Pot. Heat the oil and sauté the garlic, potatoes, parsnip, carrot, celery, and leek until they have softened.
2. Now, add in the tomato paste, water, bouillon cubes, cannellini beans, elbow pasta, oregano, basil, fennel seeds, freshly cracked black pepper, and sea salt.
3. Secure the lid. Choose the "Manual" mode and cook for 9 minutes at high pressure. Once cooking is complete, use a quick pressure release; carefully remove the lid.
4. Serve with fresh Italian parsley. Bon appétit!

Chicken Spinach and Artichoke Stuffed Spaghetti Squash

NUTRITION: CAL: 223, PROTEIN: 10.2 G, CARBS: 23.3 G, FAT: 10.9 G

10'

23'

4

INGREDIENTS

- 4 oz reduced-fat cream cheese, cubed and softened
- ¼ teaspoon ground pepper
- 3 tablespoons water
- ¼ teaspoon salt
- Crushed red peppers to serve
- 3 pounds spaghetti squash, halved lengthwise and seeded
- ½ cup shredded parmesan cheese
- 5 oz pack baby spinach
- 10 oz pack artichoke hearts, chopped
- Diced fresh basil to serve

DIRECTIONS

1. On a microwaveable dish, place your squash halves with the cut side facing up. Add 2 tablespoons of water to the squash. Set the microwave to high and cook without covering the dish for about 15 minutes. You can also place the squash on a prepared baking sheet (rimmed) and bake at 400°F for 40 minutes.
2. Set your stove to medium heat and place a large skillet containing 1 tablespoon of water on it. Add spinach into the pan and stir while it cooks for about 5 minutes, or until the vegetable wilts. Drain the spinach and place it in a bowl.
3. Place the rack in the upper third region of your oven, then preheat your broiler.
4. Using a fork, scrape the squash from each shell in half and place them in a bowl. Add artichoke hearts, pepper, salt, cream cheese, and ¼ cup parmesan into the bowl of squash. Mix well. Place squash shells on a baking sheet, and add the squash mixture into the shells. Add the remaining parmesan on top and broil for 3 minutes.
5. Garnish with red pepper and basil, and serve.

131

Angel Hair with Asparagus-Kale Pesto

NUTRITION: CALORIES: 283; FAT: 12 G; CARBS: 33 G; PROTEIN: 10 G

10'

10'

6

INGREDIENTS

- ¾ pound asparagus, woody ends removed, and coarsely chopped
- ¼ pound kale, thoroughly washed
- ½ cup grated Asiago cheese
- ¼ cup fresh basil
- ¼ cup extra-virgin olive oil
- Juice of 1 lemon
- Sea salt
- Freshly ground black pepper
- 1-pound angel hair pasta
- Zest of 1 lemon

DIRECTIONS

1. In a food processor, pulse the asparagus and kale until very finely chopped.
2. Add the Asiago cheese, basil, olive oil, and lemon juice and pulse to form a smooth pesto.
3. Season with sea salt and pepper and set aside.
4. Cook the pasta al dente according to the package directions. Drain and transfer to a large bowl.
5. Add the pesto, tossing well to coat
6. Sprinkle with lemon zest and serve.
7. Cooking tip: You can make the asparagus pesto up to 3 days ahead. Keep it refrigerated until you need it.

132

Spicy Pasta Puttanesca

NUTRITION: CALORIES: 303; FAT: 6 G; CARBS: 54 G; PROTEIN: 9 G

10'

20'

4

INGREDIENTS

- 2 teaspoons extra-virgin olive oil
- ½ sweet onion, finely chopped
- 2 teaspoons minced garlic
- 1 (28 oz) can sodium-free diced tomatoes
- ½ cup chopped anchovies
- 2 teaspoons chopped fresh oregano
- 2 teaspoons chopped fresh basil
- ½ teaspoon red pepper flakes
- ½ cup quartered Kalamata olives
- ¼ cup sodium-free chicken broth
- 1 tablespoon capers, drained and rinsed
- Juice of 1 lemon
- 4 cups cooked whole-grain penne

DIRECTIONS

1. In a large saucepan over medium heat, heat the olive oil.
2. Add the onion and garlic, and sauté for about 3 minutes until softened.
3. Stir in the tomatoes, anchovies, oregano, basil, and red pepper flakes. Bring the sauce to a boil and reduce the heat to low. Simmer for 15 minutes, stirring occasionally.
4. Stir in the olives, chicken broth, capers, and lemon juice.
5. Cook the pasta according to the package directions and serve topped with the sauce.

Ingredient tip: Do not mistake sardines for anchovies, although they are both small, silvery fish sold in cans. Anchovies are usually salted in brine and matured to create a distinctive, rich taste.

Chicken Pizza

NUTRITION: CALORIES: 393, FAT: 22 G, CARBS: 20.6 G, PROTEIN: 28.9 G

INGREDIENTS

- 2 flatbreads
- 1 tablespoon Greek vinaigrette
- ½ cup feta cheese, crumbled
- ¼ cup Parmesan cheese, grated
- ½ cup water-packed artichoke hearts, rinsed, drained and chopped
- ½ cup olives, pitted and sliced
- ½ cup cooked chicken breast strips, chopped
- ⅛ teaspoon dried basil
- ⅛ teaspoon dried oregano
- Pinch of ground black pepper
- 1 cup part-skim mozzarella cheese, shredded

DIRECTIONS

1. Preheat the oven to 400°F.
2. Arrange the flatbreads onto a large ungreased baking sheet and coat each with vinaigrette.
3. Top with feta, followed by the Parmesan, veggies and chicken.
4. Sprinkle with dried herbs and black pepper.
5. Top with mozzarella cheese evenly.
6. Bake for about 8-10 minutes or until cheese is melted.
7. Remove from the oven and set aside for about 1-2 minutes before slicing.
8. Cut each flatbread into 2 pieces and serve.

Spinach and Feta Pita Bake

NUTRITION: CALORIES: 350, PROTEIN: 11.6 G, FAT: 17.1 G

INGREDIENTS

- 6 oz sun-dried tomato pesto
- 2 chopped roma - plum tomatoes
- whole-wheat pita bread (six 6-inch)
- 1 bunch spinach
- 4 sliced mushrooms
- 2 tablespoons grated parmesan cheese
- ½ cup crumbled feta cheese
- 3 tablespoons olive oil
- Black pepper as desired

DIRECTIONS

1. Set the oven to 350°F.
2. Spread the pesto onto one side of each pita bread and arrange them onto a baking tray (pesto-side up).
3. Rinse and chop the spinach. Top the pitas with spinach, mushrooms, tomatoes, feta cheese, pepper, Parmesan cheese, pepper, and a drizzle of oil.
4. Bake in the hot oven until the pita bread is crispy (12 min.). Slice the pitas into quarters.

Beef Pizza

NUTRITION: CALORIES: 309, FAT: 3.3 G, CARBS: 36.4 G, PROTEIN: 21.4 G

25'

50'

10

INGREDIENTS

For Crust:
- 3 cups all-purpose flour
- 1 tablespoon sugar
- 2¼ teaspoons active dry yeast
- 1 teaspoon salt
- 2 tablespoons olive oil
- 1 cup warm water

For Topping:
- 1-pound ground beef
- 1 medium onion, chopped
- 2 tablespoons tomato paste
- 1 tablespoon ground cumin
- Salt and ground black pepper, as required
- ¼ cup water
- 1 cup fresh spinach, chopped
- 8 oz artichoke hearts, quartered
- 4 oz fresh mushrooms, sliced
- 2 tomatoes, chopped
- 4 oz feta cheese, crumbled

DIRECTIONS

1. For crust: in the bowl of a stand mixer, fitted with the dough hook, add the flour, sugar, yeast and salt.
2. Add 2 tablespoons of the oil and warm water and knead until a smooth and elastic dough is formed.
3. Make a ball of the dough and set aside for about 15 minutes.
4. Place the dough onto a lightly floured surface and roll into a circle.
5. Place the dough into a lightly, greased round pizza pan and gently, press to fit.
6. Set aside for about 10-15 minutes.
7. Coat the crust with some oil.
8. Preheat the oven to 400°F.
9. For topping: heat a nonstick skillet over medium-high heat and cook the beef for about 4-5 minutes.
10. Add the onion and cook for about 5 minutes, stirring frequently.
11. Add the tomato paste, cumin, salt, black pepper and water and stir to combine.
12. Reduce the heat to medium and cook for about 5-10 minutes.
13. Remove from the heat and set aside.
14. Place the beef mixture over the pizza crust and top with the spinach, followed by the artichokes, mushrooms, tomatoes, and Feta cheese.
15. Bake for about 25-30 minutes or until the cheese is melted.
16. Remove from the oven and set aside for about 3-5 minutes before slicing.
17. Cut into slices at desired size and serve.

Shrimp Pizza

NUTRITION: CALORIES: 482, FAT: 18.9 G, FAT: 7.8 G, CARBS: 44.5 G, PROTEIN: 33.4 G

15'

10'

1

INGREDIENTS

- 2 tablespoons spaghetti sauce
- 1 tablespoon pesto sauce
- 1 (6-inch) pita bread
- 2 tablespoons mozzarella cheese, shredded
- 5 cherry tomatoes, halved
- ⅛ cup bay shrimp
- Pinch of garlic powder
- Pinch of dried basil

DIRECTIONS

1. Preheat the oven to 325°F. Lightly, grease a baking sheet.
2. In a bowl, mix together the spaghetti sauce and pesto.
3. Spread the pesto mixture over the pita bread in a thin layer.
4. Top the pita bread with the cheese, followed by the tomatoes and shrimp.
5. Sprinkle with the garlic powder and basil.
6. Arrange the pita bread onto the prepared baking sheet and bake for about 7-10 minutes.
7. Remove from the oven and set aside for about 3-5 minutes before slicing.
8. Cut into desired-sized slices and serve.

Veggie Pizza

NUTRITION: CALORIES: 381, FAT: 16.1 G, FAT: 9.8 G, CARBS: 42.4 G, PROTEIN: 19.4 G

20'

12'

6

INGREDIENTS

- 1 (12-inch) prepared pizza crust
- ¼ teaspoon Italian seasoning
- ¼ teaspoon red pepper flakes, crushed
- 1 cup goat cheese, crumbled
- 1 (14-ounce) can quartered artichoke hearts
- 3 plum tomatoes, sliced into ¼-inch thick size
- 6 kalamata olives, pitted and sliced
- ¼ cup fresh basil, chopped

DIRECTIONS

1. Preheat the oven to 450°F. Grease a baking sheet.
2. Sprinkle the pizza crust with Italian seasoning and red pepper flakes evenly.
3. Place the goat cheese over the crust evenly, leaving about ½-inch of the sides.
4. With the back of a spoon, gently press the cheese downwards.
5. Place the artichoke, tomato and olives on top of the cheese.
6. Arrange the pizza crust onto the prepared baking sheet.
7. Bake for about 10-12 minutes or till cheese becomes bubbly.
8. Remove from the oven and sprinkle with the basil.
9. Cut into equal-sized wedges and serve.

138

Watermelon Feta and Balsamic Pizza

NUTRITION: PROTEIN: 2 G, FAT: 3 G, CALORIES: 90

5'

15'

INGREDIENTS

- Watermelon (1-inch thick from the center)
- Crumbled feta cheese (1 oz)
- Sliced Kalamata olives (5-6)
- Mint leaves (1 teaspoon)
- Balsamic glaze (½ tablespoon)

DIRECTIONS

1. Slice the widest section of the watermelon in half. Then, slice each half into four wedges.
2. Serve on a round pie dish like a pizza round and cover with the olives, cheese, mint leaves, and glaze.

4

139

White Pizza with Prosciutto and Arugula

NUTRITION: CALORIES: 73; PROTEIN: 12.3 G; CARBS: 3.4 G; FAT: 6.3 G

10'

15'

INGREDIENTS

- 1 pound prepared pizza dough
- ½ cup ricotta cheese
- 1 tablespoon garlic, minced
- 1 cup grated mozzarella cheese
- 3 oz prosciutto, thinly sliced
- ½ cup fresh arugula
- ½ teaspoon freshly ground black pepper

DIRECTIONS

1. Preheat the oven to 450°F. Roll out the pizza dough on a floured surface.
2. Put the pizza dough on a parchment-lined baking sheet or pizza sheet. Put the dough in the oven and bake for 8 minutes.
3. In a small bowl, mix together the ricotta, garlic, and mozzarella.
4. Remove the pizza dough from the oven and spread the cheese mixture over the top. Bake for another 5 to 6 minutes.
5. Top the pizza with prosciutto, arugula, and pepper; serve warm.

6

Za'atar Pizza

NUTRITION: CALORIES: 53; PROTEIN: 10.3 G; CARBS: 3.4 G; FAT: 6.3 G

10'

15'

5

INGREDIENTS
- 1 sheet puff pastry
- ¼ cup extra-virgin olive oil
- ⅓ cup za'atar seasoning

DIRECTIONS
- Preheat the oven to 350°F.
- Put the puff pastry on a parchment-lined baking sheet. Cut the pastry into desired slices.
- Brush the pastry with olive oil. Sprinkle with the za'atar.
- Put the pastry in the oven and bake for 10 to 12 minutes or until the edges are lightly browned and puffed up. Serve warm or at room temperature.

CHAPTER 8

Dessert recipes

141

Traditional Olive Oil Cake with Figs

NUTRITION: CALORIES: 339; FAT: 15.6 G; CARBS: 44.7 G; PROTEIN: 6.4 G

45'

0'

2

INGREDIENTS

- ½-pound cooking apples, peeled, cored, and chopped
- 2 tablespoons fresh lemon juice
- 2 ½ cups all-purpose flour
- 1 teaspoon baking powder
- ¼ teaspoon sea salt
- ½ teaspoon ground cinnamon
- A pinch of grated nutmeg
- ¾ cup granulated sugar
- ½ cup extra-virgin olive oil
- 2 eggs
- ½ cup dried figs, chopped
- 2 tablespoons walnuts, chopped

DIRECTIONS

1. Begin by preheating your oven to 350°F.
2. Toss the chopped apples with lemon juice and set them aside.
3. Then, thoroughly combine the flour, baking powder, sea salt, cinnamon, and nutmeg.
4. Then, beat the sugar and olive oil using your mixer at low speed.
5. Gradually fold in the eggs, one at a time, and continue to mix for a few minutes more until it has thickened.
6. Add the wet mixture to the dry ingredients and stir until you get a thick batter. Fold in the figs and walnuts and stir to combine well.
7. Spoon the batter into a parchment-lined baking pan and level the top using a wooden spoon.
8. Bake in the preheated oven for about 40 minutes or until the tester comes out dry and clean. Let it cool on a wire rack before slicing and serving. Bon appétit!

142

Mascarpone and Fig Crostini

NUTRITION: CALORIES: 445, FAT: 24 G, CARBS: 48 G, PROTEIN: 3 G

10'

10'

6-8

INGREDIENTS

- 1 long French baguette
- 4 tablespoons (½ stick) salted butter, melted
- 1 (8-ounce) tub mascarpone cheese
- 1 (12-ounce) jar fig jam or preserves

DIRECTIONS

1. Preheat the oven to 350°F. Slice the bread into ¼-inch-thick slices. Lay out the sliced bread on a single baking sheet and brush each slice with the melted butter.
2. Put the single baking sheet in the oven and toast the bread for 5 to 7 minutes, just until golden brown.
3. Let the bread cool slightly. Spread about a teaspoon or so of the mascarpone cheese on each piece of bread. Top with a teaspoon or so of the jam. Serve immediately.

Traditional Mediterranean Lokum

NUTRITION: CALORIES: 208; FAT: 0.5 G; CARBS: 54.4 G; PROTEIN: 0.2 G

25'

0'

20

INGREDIENTS

- 1-ounce confectioners' sugar
- 3 ½ oz cornstarch
- 20 oz caster sugar
- 4 oz pomegranate juice
- 16 oz cold water
- 3 tablespoons gelatin, powdered

DIRECTIONS

1. Line a baking sheet with parchment paper.
2. Mix the confectioners' sugar and 2 oz of cornstarch until well combined.
3. In a saucepan, heat the caster sugar, pomegranate juice and water over low heat.
4. In a mixing bowl, combine 4 oz of cold water with the remaining cornstarch. Stir the mixture into the sugar syrup.
5. Slowly and gradually, add in the powdered gelatin and whisk until smooth and uniform.
6. Bring the mixture to a boil, turn the heat to medium and continue to cook for another 18 minutes, whisking constantly, until the mixture has thickened.
7. Scrape the mixture into the baking sheet and allow it to set in your refrigerator.
8. Cut your lokum into cubes and coat with the confectioners' sugar mixture. Bon appétit!

Mixed Berry and Fig Compote

NUTRITION: CALORIES: 150; FAT: 0.5 G; CARBS: 36.4 G; PROTEIN: 1.4 G

20'

0'

5

INGREDIENTS

- 2 cups mixed berries
- 1 cup figs, chopped
- 4 tablespoons pomegranate juice
- ½ teaspoon ground cinnamon
- ½ teaspoon crystallized ginger
- ½ teaspoon vanilla extract
- 2 tablespoons honey

DIRECTIONS

1. Place the fruit, pomegranate juice, ground cinnamon, crystallized ginger, and vanilla extract in a saucepan; bring to medium heat.
2. Turn the heat to a simmer and continue to cook for about 11 minutes, stirring occasionally to combine well. Add in the honey and stir to combine.
3. Remove from the heat and keep it in your refrigerator. Bon appétit!

145

Creamed Fruit Salad

NUTRITION: CALORIES: 250; FAT: 0.7 G; CARBS: 60 G; PROTEIN: 6.4 G

10'

0'

2

INGREDIENTS

- 1 orange, peeled and sliced
- 2 apples, pitted and diced
- 2 peaches, pitted and diced
- 1 cup seedless grapes
- ¾ cup Greek-style yogurt, well-chilled
- 3 tablespoons honey

DIRECTIONS

1. Divide the fruits between dessert bowls.
2. Top with the yogurt. Add a few drizzles of honey to each serving and serve well-chilled.
3. Bon appétit!

146

Almond Cookies

NUTRITION: CALORIES: 604, FAT: 36 G, CARBS: 63 G, PROTEIN: 11 G

5'

10'

4-6

INGREDIENTS

- ½ cup sugar
- 8 tablespoons (1 stick) room temperature salted butter
- 1 large egg
- 1 ½ cup all-purpose flour
- 1 cup ground almonds or almond flour

DIRECTIONS

1. Preheat the oven to 375°F. Using a mixer, cream together the sugar and butter. Add the egg and mix until combined.
2. Alternately add the flour and ground almonds, ½ cup at a time, while the mixer is on slow.
3. Once everything is combined, line a baking sheet with parchment paper. Drop a tablespoon of dough on the baking sheet, keeping the cookies at least 2 inches apart.
4. Put the single baking sheet in the oven and bake just until the cookies start to turn brown around the edges for about 5 to 7 minutes.

147

Crunchy Sesame Cookies

NUTRITION: CALORIES: 218, FAT: 12 G, CARBS: 25 G, PROTEIN: 4 G

10'

15'

14-16

INGREDIENTS
- 1 cup sesame seeds, hulled
- 1 cup sugar
- 8 tablespoons (1 stick) salted butter, softened
- 2 large eggs
- 1¼ cups flour

DIRECTIONS
1. Preheat the oven to 350°F. Toast the sesame seeds on a baking sheet for 3 minutes. Set aside and let cool.
2. Using a mixer, cream together the sugar and butter. Put the eggs one at a time until well-blended. Add the flour and toasted sesame seeds and mix until well-blended.
3. Drop a spoonful of cookie dough onto a baking sheet and form them into round balls, about 1-inch in diameter, similar to a walnut.
4. Put in the oven and bake for 5 to 7 minutes or until golden brown. Let the cookies cool and enjoy.

148

Mini Orange Tarts

NUTRITION: CALORIES: 398; FAT: 28.5 G; CARBS: 24.9 G; PROTEIN: 11.9 G

45'

0'

2

INGREDIENTS
- 1 cup coconut flour
- ½ cup almond flour
- A pinch of grated nutmeg
- A pinch of sea salt
- ¼ teaspoon ground cloves
- ¼ teaspoon ground anise
- 1 cup brown sugar
- 6 eggs
- 2 cups heavy cream
- 2 oranges, peeled and sliced

DIRECTIONS
1. Begin by preheating your oven to 350°F.
2. Thoroughly combine the flour with spices. Stir in the sugar, eggs, and heavy cream. Mix again to combine well.
3. Divide the batter into six lightly greased ramekins.
4. Top with the oranges and bake in the preheated oven for about 40 minutes until the clafoutis is just set. Bon appétit!

149

Traditional Kalo Prama

NUTRITION: CALORIES: 478; FAT: 22.5 G; CARBS: 62.4 G; PROTEIN: 8.2 G

45'

0'

2

INGREDIENTS
- 2 large eggs
- ½ cup Greek yogurt
- ½ cup coconut oil
- ½ cup sugar
- 8 oz semolina
- 1 teaspoon baking soda
- 2 tablespoons walnuts, chopped
- ¼ teaspoon ground nutmeg
- ¼ teaspoon ground anise
- ½ teaspoon ground cinnamon
- 1 cup water
- 1 ½ cups caster sugar
- 1 teaspoon lemon zest
- 1 teaspoon lemon juice

DIRECTIONS
1. Thoroughly combine the eggs, yogurt, coconut oil, and sugar. Add in the semolina, baking soda, walnuts, nutmeg, anise, and cinnamon.
2. Let it rest for 1 ½ hour.
3. Bake in the preheated oven at 350°F for approximately 40 minutes or until a tester inserted in the center of the cake comes out dry and clean.
4. Transfer to a wire rack to cool completely before slicing.
5. Meanwhile, bring the water and caster sugar to a full boil; add in the lemon zest and lemon juice, and turn the heat to a simmer; let it simmer for about 8 minutes or until the sauce has thickened slightly.
6. Cut the cake into diamonds and pour the syrup over the top; allow it to soak for about 2 hours. Bon appétit!

150

Turkish-Style Chocolate Halva

NUTRITION: CALORIES: 388; FAT: 27.5 G; CARBS: 31.6 G; PROTEIN: 7.9 G

20'

0'

2

INGREDIENTS
- ½ cup water
- 2 cups sugar
- 2 cups tahini
- ¼ teaspoon cardamom
- ¼ teaspoon cinnamon
- A pinch of sea salt
- 6 oz dark chocolate, broken into chunks

DIRECTIONS
1. Bring the water to a full boil in a small saucepan. Add in the sugar and stir. Let it cook, stirring occasionally, until a candy thermometer registers 250°F. Heat off.
2. Stir in the tahini. Continue to stir with a wooden spoon just until halva comes together in a smooth mass; do not overmix your halva.
3. Add in the cardamom, cinnamon, and salt; stir again to combine well. Now, scrape your halva into a parchment-lined square pan.
4. Microwave the chocolate until melted; pour the melted chocolate over your halva and smooth the top.
5. Let it cool to room temperature; cover tightly with a plastic wrap and place in your refrigerator for at least 2 hours. Bon appétit!

Rice Pudding with Dried Figs

NUTRITION: CALORIES: 228; FAT: 6.1 G; CARBS: 35.1 G; PROTEIN: 7.1 G

45'

0'

2

INGREDIENTS
- 3 cups milk
- 1 cup water
- 2 tablespoons sugar
- ⅓ cup white rice, rinsed
- 1 tablespoon honey
- 4 dried figs, chopped
- ½ teaspoon cinnamon
- ½ teaspoon rose water

DIRECTIONS
1. In a deep saucepan, bring the milk, water and sugar to a boil until the sugar has dissolved.
2. Stir in the rice, honey, figs, raisins, and cinnamon, and turn the heat to a simmer; let it simmer for about 40 minutes, stirring periodically to prevent your pudding from sticking.
3. Afterward, stir in the rose water. Divide the pudding between individual bowls and serve. Bon appétit!

Fruit Kabobs with Yogurt Deep

NUTRITION: CALORIES: 98; FAT: 0.2 G; CARBS: 20.7 G; PROTEIN: 2.8 G

10'

0'

2

INGREDIENTS
- 8 clementine orange segments
- 8 medium-sized strawberries
- 8 pineapple cubes
- 8 seedless grapes
- ½ cup Greek-style yogurt
- ½ teaspoon vanilla extract
- 2 tablespoons honey

DIRECTIONS
1. Thread the fruits onto 4 skewers.
2. In a mixing dish, thoroughly combine the yogurt, vanilla, and honey.
3. Serve alongside your fruit kabobs for dipping. Bon appétit!

Stuffed Dried Figs

NUTRITION: CALORIES: 110, CARBS: 26 G, FAT: 3 G, PROTEIN: 1 G

20'

0'

4

INGREDIENTS

- 12 dried figs
- 2 tablespoons thyme honey
- 2 tablespoons sesame seeds
- 24 walnut halves

DIRECTIONS

1. Cut off the tough stalk ends of the figs.
2. Slice open each fig.
3. Stuff the fig openings with two walnut halves and close
4. Arrange the figs on a plate, drizzle with honey, and sprinkle the sesame seeds on it.
5. Serve.

Feta Cheesecake

NUTRITION: CALORIES: 98, CARBS: 7 G, FAT: 7 G, PROTEIN: 3 G

30'

90'

12

INGREDIENTS

- 2 cups graham cracker crumbs (about 30 crackers)
- ½ teaspoon ground cinnamon
- 6 tablespoons unsalted butter, melted
- ½ cup sesame seeds, toasted
- 12 oz cream cheese, softened
- 1 cup crumbled feta cheese
- 3 large eggs
- 1 cup of sugar
- 2 cups plain yogurt
- 2 tablespoons grated lemon zest
- 1 teaspoon vanilla

DIRECTIONS

1. Set the oven to 350°F.
2. Mix the cracker crumbs, butter, cinnamon, and sesame seeds with a fork. Move the combination to a springform pan and spread until it is even. Refrigerate.
3. In a separate bowl, mix the cream cheese and feta. With an electric mixer, beat both kinds of cheese together. Add the eggs one after the other, beating the mixture with each new addition. Add sugar, then keep beating until creamy. Mix in yogurt, vanilla, and lemon zest.
4. Bring out the refrigerated springform and spread the batter on it. Then place it in a baking pan. Pour water into the pan till it is halfway full.
5. Bake for about 50 minutes. Remove cheesecake and allow it to cool. Refrigerate for at least 4 hours.
6. It is done. Serve when ready.

155

No-Bake Chocolate Squares

NUTRITION: CALORIES: 198; FAT: 13 G; CARBS: 17.3 G; PROTEIN: 4.6 G

INGREDIENTS

- 8 oz bittersweet chocolate
- 1 cup tahini paste
- ¼ cup almonds, chopped
- ¼ cup walnuts, chopped

DIRECTIONS

1. Microwave the chocolate for about 30 seconds or until melted. Stir in the tahini, almonds, and walnuts.
2. Spread the batter into a parchment-lined baking pan. Place in your refrigerator until set, for about 3 hours.
3. Cut into squares and serve well-chilled. Bon appétit!

10'

0'

2

156

Greek Parfait with Mixed Berries

NUTRITION: CALORIES: 238; FAT: 16.7 G; CARBS: 53 G; PROTEIN: 21.6 G

INGREDIENTS

- 2 cups Greek yogurt
- 2 cups mixed berries
- ½ cup granola

DIRECTIONS

1. Alternate layers of mixed berries, granola, and yogurt until two dessert bowls are filled completely.
2. Cover and place in your refrigerator until you're ready to serve. Bon appétit!

10'

0'

2

Greek-Style Chocolate Semifreddo

NUTRITION: CALORIES: 517; FAT: 27.7 G; CARBS: 61 G; PROTEIN: 6.8 G

15'

0'

2

INGREDIENTS

- 3 oz dark chocolate, broken into chunks
- 1 teaspoon vanilla extract
- A pinch of grated nutmeg
- A pinch of sea salt
- 1 cup heavy cream, divided
- 2 egg whites, at room temperature
- ½ cup caster sugar
- 4 tablespoons water
- ½ cup plain Greek yogurt
- 1 tablespoon brandy
- 2 tablespoons dark chocolate curls, to decorate

DIRECTIONS

1. In a glass bowl, thoroughly combine the chocolate, vanilla, nutmeg, and sea salt.
2. In a small saucepan, bring the cream to a simmer. Pour the hot cream over the chocolate mixture and stir until everything is well incorporated.
3. Place in your refrigerator for about 1 hour.
4. Now, mix the egg whites on high speed until soft peaks form.
5. Dissolve the sugar in water over medium-low heat until a candy thermometer registers 250°F or until the syrup has thickened.
6. Now, pour the syrup into the beaten egg whites and continue to beat until glossy. Fold in the chilled chocolate mixture, Greek yogurt, and brandy; mix again until everything is well combined.
7. Freeze your dessert for at least 3 hours. Then, let it sit at room temperature for about 15 minutes before slicing and serving. Top with the chocolate curls. Bon appétit!

158

Traditional Italian Cake with Almonds

NUTRITION: CALORIES: 407; FAT: 14.7 G; CARBS: 61.4 G; PROTEIN: 6.6 G

45'

0'

2

INGREDIENTS

- 4 ripe peaches, peeled, pitted, and sliced
- 1 tablespoon fresh lemon juice
- 2 ¼ cups all-purpose flour
- 1 teaspoon baking soda
- ½ teaspoon baking powder
- A pinch of grated nutmeg
- A pinch of sea salt
- ½ teaspoon ground cloves
- ½ teaspoon ground cinnamon
- ½ cup olive oil
- 1 ⅓ cups sugar
- 3 eggs, at room temperature
- 1 cup Greek yogurt
- 1 teaspoon pure vanilla extract
- ½ cup almonds, chopped

DIRECTIONS

1. Begin by preheating your oven to 350°F. Toss the peaches with lemon juice and set them aside.
2. Then, thoroughly combine the dry ingredients.
3. Then, beat the olive oil and sugar using your mixer at low speed.
4. Gradually fold in the eggs, one at a time, and continue to mix for a few minutes more until it has thickened. Add in the yogurt and vanilla, and mix again.
5. Add the wet mixture to the dry ingredients and stir until you get a thick batter. Fold in the almonds and stir to combine well.
6. Spoon the batter into a parchment-lined baking pan and level the top using a wooden spoon.
7. Bake in the preheated oven for about 40 minutes or until a tester comes out dry and clean. Let it cool on a wire rack before slicing and serving. Bon appétit!

159

Pear Croustade

NUTRITION: CALORIES: 498, CARBS: 32 G, FAT: 32 G, PROTEIN: 18 G

30'

60'

10

INGREDIENTS

- 1 cup + 1 tablespoon all-purpose flour, divided
- 4 ½ tablespoons sugar, divided
- ⅛ teaspoon salt
- 6 tablespoons unsalted butter, chilled, cut into ½-inch cubes
- 1 large-sized egg, separated
- 1 ½ tablespoon ice-cold water
- 3 firm, ripe pears (Bosc), peeled, cored, sliced into ¼-inch slices 1 tablespoon fresh lemon juice
- ⅓ teaspoon ground allspice
- 1 teaspoon anise seeds

DIRECTIONS

1. Pour 1 cup of flour, 1 ½ tablespoon of sugar, butter, and salt into a food processor and combine the ingredients by pulsing.
2. Whisk the yolk of the egg and ice water in a separate bowl. Mix the egg mixture with the flour mixture. It will form a dough, wrap it, and set aside for an hour.
3. Set the oven to 400°F.
4. Mix the pear, sugar, leftover flour, allspice, anise seed, and lemon juice in a large bowl to make a filling.
5. Arrange the filling in the center of the dough.
6. Bake for about 40 minutes. Cool for about 15 minutes before serving.

160

Loukoumades (Fried Honey Balls)

NUTRITION: CALORIES: 355, CARBS: 64 G, FAT: 7 G, PROTEIN: 6 G

20'

45'

10

INGREDIENTS
- 2 cups sugar
- 1 cup water
- 1 cup honey
- 1 ½ cup tepid water
- 1 tablespoon brown sugar
- ¼ cup vegetable oil
- 1 tablespoon active dry yeast
- 1 ½ cups all-purpose flour, 1 cup cornstarch, ½ teaspoon salt
- Vegetable oil for frying
- 1 ½ cup chopped walnuts
- ¼ cup ground cinnamon

DIRECTIONS
1. Boil the sugar and water on medium heat. Add honey after 10 minutes. Cool and set aside.
2. Mix the tepid water, oil, brown sugar, and yeast in a large bowl. Allow it to sit for 10 minutes. In a distinct bowl, blend the flour, salt, and cornstarch. With your hands mix the yeast and the flour to make a wet dough. Cover and set aside for 2 hours.
3. Fry in oil at 350°F. Use your palm to measure the sizes of the pieces of dough as they are dropped into the frying pan. Fry each batch for about 3-4 minutes.
4. Immediately after the loukoumades are done frying, drop them in the prepared syrup.
5. Serve with cinnamon and walnuts.

161

Creme Caramel

NUTRITION: CALORIES: 110, CARBS: 21 G, FAT: 1 G, PROTEIN: 2 G

60'

60'

12

INGREDIENTS
- 5 cups whole milk
- 2 teaspoons vanilla extract
- 8 large egg yolks
- 4 large-sized eggs
- 2 cups sugar, divided
- ¼ cup water

DIRECTIONS
1. Preheat the oven to 350°F
2. Heat the milk with medium heat and wait for it to be scalded.
3. Mix 1 cup of sugar and egg yolks in a bowl and add to the eggs.
4. With a nonstick pan on high heat, boil the water and remaining sugar. Do not stir, instead whirl the pan. When the sugar forms caramel, divide it into ramekins.
5. Divide the egg mixture into the ramekins and place them in a baking pan. Increase water to the pan until it is half full. Bake for 30 minutes.
6. Remove the ramekins from the baking pan, cool, then refrigerate for at least 8 hours.
7. Serve.

162

Galaktoboureko

NUTRITION: CALORIES: 393, CARBS: 55 G, FAT: 15 G, PROTEIN: 8 G

30'

90'

12

INGREDIENTS

- 4 cups sugar, divided
- 1 tablespoon fresh lemon juice
- 1 cup water
- 1 tablespoon plus 1 ½ teaspoon grated lemon zest, divided into 10 cups
- 1 cup Room temperature whole milk
- 1 cup + 2 tablespoons unsalted butter, melted and divided into 2
- 2 Tablespoons vanilla extract
- 7 large-sized eggs
- 1 cup fine semolina
- 1 package phyllo, thawed and at room temperature

DIRECTIONS

1. Preheat the oven to 350°F
2. Mix 2 cups of sugar, lemon juice, 1 ½ teaspoon of lemon zest, and water. Boil over medium heat. Set aside.
3. Mix the milk, 2 Tablespoons of butter, and vanilla in a pot and put on medium heat. Remove from heat when milk is scalded
4. Mix the eggs and semolina in a bowl, then add the mixture to the scalded milk. Put the egg-milk mixture on medium heat. Stir until it forms a custard-like material.
5. Brush butter on each sheet then arrange all over the baking pan until everywhere is covered. Spread the custard on the bottom pile of phyllo
6. Arrange the buttered phyllo all over the top of the custard until every inch is covered.
7. Bake for about 40 minutes. Cover the top of the pie with all the prepared syrup. Serve.

163

Kourabiedes Almond Cookies

NUTRITION: CALORIES: 102, CARBS: 10 G, FAT: 7 G, PROTEIN: 2 G

20'

50'

20

INGREDIENTS

- 1 ½ cups unsalted butter, clarified, at room temperature 2 cups
- 2 cups Confectioners' sugar, divided
- 1 large egg yolk
- 2 tablespoons brandy
- 1 ½ teaspoon baking powder
- 1 teaspoon vanilla extract
- 5 cups all-purpose flour, sifted
- 1 cup roasted almonds, chopped

DIRECTIONS

1. Preheat the oven to 350°F
2. Thoroughly mix butter and ½ cup of sugar in a bowl. Add in the egg after a while. Create a brandy mixture by mixing the brandy and baking powder. Add the mixture to the egg, add vanilla, then keep beating until the ingredients are properly blended
3. Add flour and almonds to make a dough.
4. Roll the dough to form crescent shapes. You should be able to get about 40 pieces. Place the pieces on a baking sheet, then bake in the oven for 25 minutes.
5. Allow the cookies to cool, then coat them with the remaining confectioner's sugar.
6. Serve.

164

Revani Syrup Cake

NUTRITION: CALORIES: 348, CARBS: 55 G, FAT: 9 G, PROTEIN: 5 G

30'

3h

24

INGREDIENTS

- 1 tablespoon unsalted butter
- 2 tablespoons all-purpose flour
- 1 cup ground rusk or bread crumbs
- 1 cup fine semolina flour
- ¾ cup ground toasted almonds
- 3 teaspoons baking powder
- 16 large eggs
- 2 tablespoons vanilla extract
- 3 cups sugar, divided
- 3 cups water
- 5 (2-inch) strips lemon peel, pith removed
- 3 tablespoons fresh lemon juice
- 1 oz brandy

DIRECTIONS

1. Preheat the oven to 350°F. Grease the baking pan with 1 tablespoon of butter and flour.
2. Mix the rusk, almonds, semolina, and baking powder in a bowl.
3. In another bowl, mix the eggs, 1 cup of sugar, and vanilla; whisk with an electric mixer for about 5 minutes. Add the semolina mixture to the eggs and stir.
4. Pour the stirred batter into the greased baking pan and place it in the preheated oven.
5. With the remaining sugar, lemon peels, and water make the syrup by boiling the mixture on medium heat. Add the lemon juice after 6 minutes, then cook for 3 minutes. Remove the lemon peels and set the syrup aside.
6. After the cake is done in the oven, spread the syrup over the cake.
7. Cut the cake as you please and serve.

165

Almonds and Oats Pudding

NUTRITION: CALORIES: 174, FAT: 12.1 G, CARBS: 3.9 G, PROTEIN: 4.8 G

10'

15'

4

INGREDIENTS

- 1 tablespoon lemon juice
- Zest of 1 lime
- 1 and ½ cups almond milk
- 1 teaspoon almond extract
- ½ cup oats
- 2 tablespoons stevia
- ½ cup silver almonds, chopped

DIRECTIONS

1. In a pan, blend the almond milk plus the lime zest and the other ingredients, whisk, bring to a simmer and cook over medium heat for 15 minutes.
2. Split the mix into bowls then serve cold.

Mediterranean Tomato Salad with Feta and Fresh Herbs

NUTRITION: CALORIES: 125, PROTEIN: 2 G, CARBS: 8 G, FAT: 9 G

10'

15'

2

INGREDIENTS

- 5 diced tomatoes
- 2 oz crumbled feta cheese
- ½ cup chopped fresh dill
- ½ cup diced onion
- 6 chopped mint leaves
- ½ teaspoon paprika
- 3 tablespoons olive oil
- 2 tablespoons minced garlic
- 2 teaspoons lemon juice
- 2 teaspoons white wine vinegar
- Salt and black pepper to taste

DIRECTIONS

1. Combine the onions, tomatoes, herbs and the garlic in a bowl, then season with your spices (salt, black pepper, paprika).
2. To create the dressing, in a separate bowl first mix together the olive oil, vinegar, and lemon juice.
3. Top with feta cheese

Quinoa Bowl with Yogurt, Dates, and Almonds

NUTRITION: CALORIES: 125, PROTEIN: 2 G, CARBS: 8 G, FAT: 9 G

10'

15'

2

INGREDIENTS

- 1 ½ cup water
- 1 cup quinoa
- 2 cinnamon sticks
- 1-inch knob of ginger, peeled
- ¼ teaspoon kosher salt
- 1 cup plain Greek yogurt
- ½ cup dates, pitted and chopped
- ½ cup almonds (raw or roasted), chopped
- 2 teaspoons honey (optional)

DIRECTIONS

1. Bring the water, quinoa, cinnamon sticks, ginger, and salt to a boil in a medium saucepan over high heat.
2. Reduce the heat to a simmer and cover; simmer for 10 to 12 minutes. Remove the cinnamon sticks and ginger. Fluff with a fork.
3. Add the yogurt, dates, and almonds to the quinoa and mix together. Divide evenly among 4 bowls and garnish with ½ teaspoon honey per bowl, if desired.
4. Use any nuts or seeds you like in place of the almonds.

168

Almond Butter Banana Chocolate Smoothie

NUTRITION: CALORIES: 125, PROTEIN: 2 G, CARBS: 8 G, FAT: 9 G

5'

30'

2

INGREDIENTS
- ¾ cup almond milk
- ½ medium banana, preferably frozen
- ¼ cup frozen blueberries
- 1 tablespoon almond butter
- 1 tablespoon unsweetened cocoa powder
- 1 tablespoon chia seeds

DIRECTIONS
1. In a blender or Vitamix, add all the ingredients. Blend to combine.
2. Peanut butter, sunflower seed butter, and other kinds of nut butter are good choices to replace the almond butter

169

Maple Vanilla Baked Pears

NUTRITION: CALORIES: 153, FAT: 6 G, CARBS: 16 G, PROTEIN: 6 G

10'

30'

4

INGREDIENTS
- 4 D'Anjou pears
- ½ cup Pure Maple Syrup (120 ml)
- ¼ teaspoon Ground cinnamon
- 1 teaspoon pure vanilla extract
- Optional toppings: Greek yogurt, maple pecan granola

DIRECTIONS
1. Preheat the oven to 190°C (375°F).
2. Cut the pears, and cut a small sliver from the underside so that when set upright on the baking sheet, the pears sit flat. Core out the seeds using a big or medium cookie scoop and melon scoop (or even a teaspoon). Arrange the pears on the baking dish, face up. Sprinkle with cinnamon uniformly- if you like, feel free to add more cinnamon.
3. In a small bowl, mix the maple syrup and vanilla extract. Drizzle much of it all over the
4. Pears, reserving only 2 tablespoons for baking after the pears are completed.
5. Bake the pears for about 25 minutes, until the sides are soft and lightly browned. Remove from the oven and drizzle instantly with any leftover mixture of maple syrup. With the granola and yogurt, serve warm. Store the leftovers for up to 5 days in the refrigerator.

170

Easy Roasted Fruit Recipe

NUTRITION: CALORIES: 256, FAT: 9 G, CARBS: 25 G, PROTEIN: 4 G

INGREDIENTS

- 4 Peaches, peeled and sliced
- 1 ½ cups Fresh blueberries
- ⅛ teaspoon Ground cinnamon
- 3 tablespoons brown sugar

DIRECTIONS

1. Preheat the oven to 350°F.
2. In a baking dish, spread the sliced peaches and blueberries. Sprinkled with brown sugar and cinnamon.
3. Bake for about 20 minutes at 350°F, then change the oven settings to a low grill and broil for about five min, or until sparkling.
4. Serve warm, cover and refrigerate, or let cool.

171

Triple Chocolate Tiramisu

NUTRITION: CALORIES: 256, FAT: 19 G, CARBS: 17 G, PROTEIN: 6 G

INGREDIENTS

- 2 3-ounce ladyfingers package, split
- ¼ cup espresso brewed or strong coffee
- 1 8 oz mascarpone carton cheese
- 1 cup whipped cream
- ¼ cup sugar powdered
- 1 teaspoon vanilla
- ⅓ cup chocolate liqueur
- 4 White baking bars of 1 ounce, grated
- 1 oz bittersweet, grated chocolate
- 4 tablespoons Unsweetened cocoa powdered
- Chopped coffee beans covered in chocolate (optional)

DIRECTIONS

1. With some of the ladyfingers, line the bottom of an 8x8x2-inch baking pan, cutting to fit as required. Drizzle over the ladyfingers with half of the espresso; set aside.
2. Beat together the mascarpone cheese, powdered sugar, whipped cream, and vanilla with an electric mixer in a medium mixing cup, only before stiff peaks develop. Up until now combined, beat in the chocolate liqueur. Spoon half of the mascarpone combination, pouring evenly around the ladyfingers. Sprinkle over the mascarpone mixture of white chocolate and bittersweet chocolate. Top with a different layer of ladyfinger (reserve any leftover ladyfingers for another use). A layer with the remaining mixture of espresso and mascarpone cheese.
3. For 6 to 24 hours, cover and chill. Sift the cocoa powder over the dessert top. Garnish with cocoa beans, if desired.
4. Make twelve squares.

Easy Strawberry Crepes Recipe

NUTRITION: CALORIES: 120, FAT: 7 G, CARBS: 18 G, PROTEIN: 6 G

10'

12'

12

INGREDIENTS

- 2 cups sliced frozen strawberries, thawed
- 2 tablespoons sugar
- ½ teaspoon orange zest, optional
- 3 cups fresh strawberries, diced
- 2 large eggs
- 2 tablespoons butter, slightly melted and cooled
- 2 cups milk
- 1 teaspoon vanilla
- 1 tablespoon sugar
- ½ teaspoon salt
- 1 ½ cups flour

DIRECTIONS

For the Straw- berry filling:

1. Gently puree the strawberries to thaw. Stir in honey, orange zest if using, and fresh sliced strawberries. Serve at room temperature with a strawberry filling.

For Crêpes:

2. In the order listed, add the ingredients to the blender jar, cover and blend until smooth.
3. Until cooking, refrigerate overnight or for 1 hour. (Or you can strain any lumps and use them immediately if you'd prefer.)
4. Over medium heat, heat the crepe pan or an 8-inch skillet and brush loosely with butter or cooking spray. Pour ¼ cup of batter into the middle of the skillet with each crepe and then roll the pan, so the batter covers the skillet's bottom with a thin layer. Cook for about 1 minute, before light brown and the top, starts to dry out. Flip and boil for an extra 30 seconds.
5. Repeat for the batter that remains. Pile the completed crepes on a tray. (Place wax paper between the crepes if the crepes hold together.) In a 200 degrees C oven, you should put crepes to stay warm before ready to serve.
6. With a strawberry filling, fill each crepe and roll up. With whipped cream, serve it.

Dried Fruit Compote

NUTRITION: CALORIES: 258, FAT: 5 G, CARBS: 8 G, PROTEIN: 4 G

5'

20'

6

INGREDIENTS
- 8 oz dried apricots, quartered
- 8 oz dried peaches, quartered
- 1 cup golden raisins
- 1 ½ cup orange juice
- 1 cinnamon stick
- 4 whole cloves

DIRECTIONS
1. Stir to merge. Close, select the Manual button, and adjust the time to 3 minutes. When the timer beeps, let the pressure release naturally for about 20 minutes. Press the Cancel button and open the lid.
2. Remove and discard cinnamon stick and cloves. Press the Sauté button and simmer for 5–6 minutes. Serve warm then cover and refrigerate for up to a week.

Chocolate Rice Pudding

NUTRITION: CALORIES: 271, FAT: 8 G, CARBS: 4 G, PROTEIN: 3 G

10'

20'

6

INGREDIENTS
- 2 cups almond milk
- 1 cup long-grain brown rice
- 2 tablespoons Dutch-processed cocoa powder
- ¼ cup maple syrup
- 1 teaspoon vanilla extract
- ½ cup chopped dark chocolate

DIRECTIONS
1. Place almond milk, rice, cocoa, maple syrup, and vanilla in the Instant Pot®. Close then select the Manual button, and set the time to 20 minutes.
2. When the timer beeps, let the pressure release naturally for 15 minutes, then quick-release the remaining pressure. Press the Cancel button and open the lid. Serve warm, sprinkled with chocolate.

175

Fruit Compote

NUTRITION: CALORIES: 211, FAT: 1 G, CARBS: 4 G, PROTEIN: 2 G

10'

15'

6

INGREDIENTS
- 1 cup apple juice
- 1 cup dry white wine
- 2 tablespoons honey
- 1 cinnamon stick
- ¼ teaspoon ground nutmeg
- 1 tablespoon grated lemon zest
- 1½ tablespoon grated orange zest
- 3 large apples, peeled, cored, and chopped
- 3 large pears, peeled, cored, and chopped
- ½ cup dried cherries

DIRECTIONS
1. Situate all ingredients in the Instant Pot® and stir well. Close and select the Manual button, and allow it to sit for 1 minute. When the timer beeps, rapidly release the pressure until the float valve hit the bottom. Click Cancel then open the lid.
2. Use a slotted spoon to transfer the fruit to a serving bowl. Remove and discard cinnamon stick. Press the Sauté button and bring juice into the pot to a boil. Cook, stirring constantly until reduced to a syrup that will coat the back of a spoon, about 10 minutes.
3. Stir syrup into the fruit mixture. Once cool slightly, then wrap with plastic and chill overnight.

Index

Simboli

5-Minute Heirloom Tomato and Cucumber Toast 52
10-Minute Mediterranean Vegan Pasta 109
15-Minute Caprese Pasta Recipe 114

A

Almond Butter Banana Chocolate Smoothie 146
Almond Cookies 134
Almonds and Oats Pudding 144
Angel Hair with Asparagus-Kale Pesto 124
Asparagus Fries 76
Authentic Pasta e Fagioli 122
Avocado and Apple Smoothie 44

B

Bacon and Cream Cheese Mug Muffins 40
Bacon and Eggs with Tomatoes 55
Baked Rolled Oat with Pears and Pecans 84
Baked Zucchini Noodles with Feta 66
Banana Waffles 78
Beef and Broccoli Roast 73
Beef and Broccoli Stir-Fry 64
Beef Pizza 126
Best Vegan Chili with Quinoa 110
Blueberry Greek Yogurt Pancakes 45
Braised Chicken with Wild Mushrooms 92
Braised Duck with Fennel Root 92
Breakfast Couscous 43
Breakfast Egg on Avocado 56
Breakfast Taco Scramble 49
Brekky Egg-Potato Hash 58
Brown Rice Pilaf with Golden Raisins 104
Brussels Sprouts with Bacon 67
Bun less Burger—Keto Style 67

C

Carrot Potato Medley 85
Cauliflower Fritters with Hummus 50
Cauliflower soufflé 78
Cheddar-Stuffed Burgers with Zucchini 62
Cheesy Amish Breakfast Casserole 43
Cheesy Cauliflower Croquettes 74
Cheesy Mushroom Slices 75

Cherry Smoothie Bowl 59
Chicken Cordon Bleu with Cauliflower 63
Chicken Gyros with Tzatziki 93
Chicken Pizza 125
Chicken Spinach and Artichoke Stuffed Spaghetti Squash 123
Chicken Tikka with Cauliflower Rice 64
Chocolate Rice Pudding 149
Cinnamon and Pecan Porridge 40
Classic Escabeche 101
Coffee BBQ Pork Belly 68
Cold Lemon Zoodles 119
Creamed Fruit Salad 134
Creamy Mango and Banana Overnight Oats 55
Crème Caramel 142
Crispy Broccoli Pop Corn 74
Crunchy Sesame Cookies 135

D

Date and Walnut Overnight Oats 46
Delicious Okra 88
Delicious Pepper Zucchini 87
Dijon and Herb Pork Tenderloin 95
Dill and Tomato Frittata 41
Dinosaur Eggs 41
Dried Fruit Compote 149
Drunken Wild Mushroom Pasta 113

E

Easy Italian Shrimp Tortellini Bake 116
Easy Roasted Fruit Recipe 147
Easy Spaghetti Squash 54
Easy Strawberry Crepes Recipe 148
Eggplant Casserole 94
Eggplant with Olives 89

F

Farfalle with Tuna, Lemon, and Fennel 116
Feta and Quinoa Egg Muffins 51
Feta Avocado and Mashed Chickpea Toast 53
Feta Cheesecake 138
Feta Green Beans 86
Fish and Orzo 103
Fish Fillet on Lemons 98

Flavors Basil Lemon Ratatouille 86
Fried Green Beans Rosemary 73
Fruit Compote 150
Fruit Kabobs with Yogurt Deep 137

G

Galaktoboureko 143
Garlic and Thyme Lamb Chops 68
Garlic Parmesan Chicken Wings 52
Greek Green Beans 84
Greek Meatballs 97
Greek Parfait with Mixed Berries 139
Greek-Style Chocolate Semifreddo 140
Greek Yogurt with Berries and Seeds 47
Grilled Pesto Salmon with Asparagus 62
Guacamole 77

H

Harissa Yogurt Chicken Thighs 91
Hearty Beef and Bacon Casserole 65

I

Ingredient Chicken Feta Pasta 108
Italian Breakfast Sausage with Baby Potatoes and Vegetables 45

J

Jamaican Jerk Pork Roast 69

K

Kale Chips 76
Kourabiedes Almond Cookies 143

L

Lamb with String Beans 97
Lemon Artichokes 87
Loaded Portobello Mushrooms 90
Loukoumades (Fried Honey Balls 142

M

Maple Vanilla Baked Pears 146
Mascarpone and Fig Crostini 132
Mediterranean Breakfast Egg White Sandwich 48
Mediterranean One-Pot Pasta 115
Mediterranean Pasta 106
Mediterranean Pasta with Basil 57
Mediterranean Tomato Salad with Feta and Fresh Herbs 145
Mini Frittatas 44

Mini Orange Tarts 135
Mixed Berry and Fig Compote 133
Mixed Vegetable Patties—Instant Pot 69

N

No-Bake Chocolate Squares 139
Nonna's Spaghetti and Broccoli 107

O

One-Pot Buffalo Chicken Pasta 112
One-Pot Creamy Hummus Pasta 107
One-Pot Creamy Tuscan Garlic Spaghetti 109
One-Pot Spinach and Feta Macaroni and Cheese 112
Overnight Berry Chia Oats 51

P

Paleo Almond Banana Pancakes 42
Parmesan-Crusted Halibut with Asparagus 65
Parsnips with Eggplant 88
Pasta Alla Norma with Eggplant, Basil and Pecorino 120
Pasta Fagioli 117
Pastry-Less Spanakopita 46
Pear and Mango Smoothie 47
Pear Croustade 141
Pilaf with Cream Cheese 53
Potato Scallops with Truffle Oil 57

Q

Quinoa Bowl with Yogurt, Dates, and Almonds 145

R

Revani Syrup Cake 144
Rice Pudding with Dried Figs 137
Ritzy Veggie Chili 82
Roasted Leg of Lamb 70
Rosemary Roasted Pork with Cauliflower 63

S

Salmon Pasta 70
Sea Bass Crusted with Moroccan Spices 100
Sesame Wings with Cauliflower 66
Shrimp and Pasta Stew 119
Shrimp Pasta with Lemon Garlic Sauce 111
Shrimp Pizza 127
Shrimp Spaghetti Aglio Olio 114
Skillet Fried Cod 71
Slow-Cooked Kalua Pork and Cabbage 71
Spiced Soup with Lentils and Legumes 103
Spicy Italian Bean Balls with Marinara 83
Spicy Pasta Puttanesca 124
Spicy Zucchini 85

Spinach and Feta Pita Bake 125
Spinach in Cheese Envelopes 75
Spinach Pesto Pasta 121
Steak Pinwheels 72
Steak with Red Wine-Mushroom Sauce 96
Stuffed Dried Figs 138
Sumac Chicken with Cauliflower and Carrots 91
Sun-Dried Tomatoes Oatmeal 56
Sweet Potato Noodles with Almond Sauce 118

T

Tangy Shrimp 72
Thyme Whole Roasted Red Snapper 102
Tilapia Fillet with Onion and Avocado 99
Tomato Stuffed with Cheese and Peppers 90
Tortellini with Pesto and Broccoli 121
Traditional Italian Cake with Almonds 141
Traditional Kalo Prama 136
Traditional Mediterranean Lokum 133
Traditional Olive Oil Cake with Figs 132

Triple Chocolate Tiramisu 147
Turkey Burgers with Mango Salsa 79
Turkish-Style Chocolate Halva 136

V

Veggie Pizza 127

W

Watermelon Feta and Balsamic Pizza 128
White Pizza with Prosciutto and Arugula 128

Z

Za'atar Pizza 129
Zucchini Noodles 77
Zucchini, Tomato, Potato Ratatouille 89
Zucchini with Egg 42

Conclusion

If you need to do something, it's important to be able to do it well. To get better at things that matter most to us, we can learn and practice. Consuming the Mediterranean diet is known to help with weight loss and other health benefits, but there are also many ways in which people can improve their diet by reading about healthful Mediterranean food options. The following blog post will touch on these points and give suggestions on how readers can enjoy a healthy Mediterranean lifestyle.

There are also many ways that people can improve their lifestyle when following the Mediterranean diet. The following are just a few ideas for those who want to achieve their weight-loss objectives.

The first thing is to pick foods that are more flavorful than you normally would. When reading the Mediterranean diet, many readers might feel compelled to always eat bland meals and snacks that don't contain much flavor. The solution to this problem is to go out and get your hands on some homemade pesto sauce and marinara sauce because both of them contain a lot of flavors but few calories. Adding these sauces to your meals will boost the taste without adding extra calories. This way, you can still enjoy your healthy food choices and it will taste great, too.

The second thing is to not be afraid to experiment. Many people shy away from trying new foods because they're afraid that they won't like them and will end up eating too much of the same foods over and over again. This happens because these people make their food choices based on what they already like instead of trying something new and trying recipes that look good on the menu.

The next point to remember is that your training routine must be quite strenuous. While being able to get enough exercise is important for overall health, a normal working out routine will work just fine when it comes to the Mediterranean diet. It's very important for people to incorporate some sort of activity into their daily schedule because a lack of physical activity increases one's risk for death from all causes during the early years of one's lifespan. This means that if you're not up and about on a regular basis, then chances are you're going to die sooner than you should. The more active you are, the longer your life will be and this is why it's so important not to skip out on your exercises.

The fourth thing that people should remember is not to become obsessed with their weight. Many people find that the first time they start following the Mediterranean diet, they end up weighing themselves very often because they're trying to keep track of how much weight they've lost. It's important for readers to remember that you shouldn't feel like you need to weigh yourself on a daily basis because it can be very frustrating if you gain weight over the weekend and your scale doesn't register the gain until Monday morning. Some scales even incorrectly measure your height so don't put too much emphasis on what your scale says about your weight loss. Instead, focus on how you feel instead of just what you weigh.

The final thing that is worth mentioning is for people to make sure not to confuse the Mediterranean diet with the Japanese diet. These two diets are very different and only share the similarities of them both being healthy. The Japanese diet is full of things like rice, noodles and seafood whereas the Mediterranean diet includes mostly Mediterranean foods such as fruits and vegetables. It's very important for readers to understand that these two diets are quite different and that if they want to try a new way of eating, then they need to be sure that it's by following a Mediterranean diet.

With all of this information available, it should be easy for people to start following the Mediterranean diet in an effort to reap all of its benefits. In fact, it's quite easy to do so because the Mediterranean diet is rich in recipes that everyone will enjoy. This means that if someone wants to try a new way of eating, they can search through a variety of different websites and blogs where they can find a wide array of healthy recipes for various types of foods in addition to one or two simple recipes that you can follow to get started on your diet. This way you'll only have to make a few changes in order to start following this diet.